WOMEN IN
AMERICAN HISTORY

When Harriet Beecher Stowe was introduced to President Lincoln, he exclaimed: "What! are you the little woman that caused this great war?"

WOMEN IN AMERICAN HISTORY

By

GRACE HUMPHREY

Essay Index Reprint Series

BOOKS FOR LIBRARIES PRESS
FREEPORT, NEW YORK

LIBRARY OF CONGRESS CATALOG CARD NUMBER:

68-57323

PRINTED IN THE UNITED STATES OF AMERICA

CONTENTS

WOMEN IN
AMERICAN HISTORY

Women in American History

CHAPTER I

POCAHONTAS

1595-1617

ONE cold stormy day, more than three hundred years ago, a group of Indians was sitting around the fire in a "long house" on the James River in Virginia. Warriors and young braves, squaws and maidens, were listening to stories, while the children played about boisterously. Some of them were wrestling, some racing with dogs, and others turning somersaults in the long narrow passageway.

Suddenly the deerskin curtains parted and in dashed an Indian runner. He spied the chief at the far end of the room near the fire and started toward him; but one of the children, a little girl named Mataoka, who was turning handsprings, collided with him and knocked him down. A little girl she was, ten or eleven years old, with swarthy skin, black eyes and long straight hair, like all the other Indian girls; but she was distinguished among the group, for she was the daughter of the chief.

"Child," said her father, "in your rough play you have knocked down your brother, the runner who has come with some message. That is not play for a girl. Why will you be such a little tomboy?"

At this all the Indians present took up the word *tomboy* and repeated it in the guttural Algonquin speech—*pocahuntas, pocahuntas.* And that nickname stayed with her all her life long.

"I have news," said the runner, when he could get his breath. "I have great news," and he paused dramatically. "The white captain is caught!"

What an excitement this created in the long house! Warriors and squaws crowded around the tired runner, eager to have the details of his story—how two hundred Indians, with the chief's brother at their head, had watched from behind the trees as the white captain, with an Indian guide, left his two men in the boat and went ashore; how stealthily they lay in wait to attack him, in the heart of the deep woods; how they shot their arrows thick and fast, when the right moment came, till they saw the white captain seize the Indian and use him as a shield, while he slowly made his way back toward the boat; how the Indians were afraid they would lose their prey after all, but fortune favored them when the white man stumbled into a bog and was held fast by the slippery ground and the icy water; and how, after he was nearly dead with the cold and had thrown away his arms, they took him prisoner. At first, said the runner, the braves wanted to kill him, but later thought it would be a better plan to lead him to the village where the whole tribe could rejoice in this triumph.

All this Pocahontas, the little daughter of the great chief Powhatan, heard, and was deeply interested. For the plucky captain had saved his life by a device that was almost an Indian trick. So you may be sure she was there, the next day, when the noted prisoner was brought in. She was very proud of her father, who ruled over a league of nearly forty tribes, numbering some eight thousand people, as she looked up at **him,** sitting in state on a raised platform, dressed in raccoon skins, with all the tails left on, and wearing his splendid crown of red feathers. Proud, too, she was to be his favorite daughter.

At the council Mataoka listened while the Indians told how the prisoner had shot at their men, one of whom had since died. She was heavy-hearted when she learned the verdict, "Then he too must die—that is the Indian custom!" She watched while some young braves brought in two great stones and placed them in front of Powhatan. She saw them seize the prisoner, drag him before her father, force him down until his head was on the stones, and then tie his hands and feet. And all the time her heart went out to him, so fair, so friendly, so fine a man he was!

Meanwhile John Smith, the white captain, not understanding what the Indians were saying, could only guess at his fate. He had often been near to death, in his adventurous life, and he thought now of some of his narrow escapes—of his fighting days in the Low Countries, in the Holy

Land against the Turks, and that wonderful day
when he met the three Turkish champions in single
combat, came out victorious, and was given a coat
of arms. He thought of the times he had been
robbed and shipwrecked, captured by Barbary pi-
rates and sold into slavery. Yes, he had been
close to death before. Would some providence
save him this time?

No, there were only forbidding looks on the
swarthy faces around him, glances of hatred,
contempt, of triumph. Smith, from his position
on the ground, saw the chief motion to the executioners, who brought in their great war clubs.
Now they swung them up over their shoulders and
stood ready for the word of command. Powhatan had opened his lips to speak when
suddenly there was a commotion in the group
as a little figure darted past the platform, slipped
through deterring hands, and flung herself on the
helpless prisoner.

No girl's game now was the little tomboy playing, as she took John Smith's head in her arms
and with her own body shielded him from death.
The executioners stopped, uncertain what to do,

for they were fond of the chief's daughter and would not harm a hair of her head. With flashing eyes she waved them back and pleaded with the stern Powhatan to spare the white captain's life.

At once there was a scene of the wildest commotion. There were shouts and threats and many cries of "Kill! Kill!" for the Indians feared the power of these newcomers and longed to drive them from the land. But the little Pocahontas was a chief's daughter and stood for her rights. Let them grant this enemy his life and adopt him into their tribe; for what harm had he done them? They ought to be friends. And she had her way. Powhatan raised his hand and when the clamor ceased, he spoke to the warriors who set the plucky paleface free.

Mataoka smiled upon him and gave him many a look of wondering curiosity. Smith presented her with some trifling gifts and asked her name. Now it was the Indian custom never to tell a name to a stranger, lest it give him some magic harmful influence, so Powhatan replied that his daughter's name was Pocahontas.

POCAHONTAS

This story is questioned by some historians because Smith did not include it in his first published account of the Virginia colony, nor yet in the second, though he did praise the Indian girl. In a letter he sent to the English queen, years later, bespeaking for her the royal favor, he tells how Pocahontas saved his life and the colony as well.

True or not, Pocahontas and Smith became warm friends and the kind-hearted little Indian girl was loyal and faithful to the settlement at Jamestown, and saved the colony more than once. Frequently she would go with her brothers, or some of her Indian attendants, carrying corn or venison to the people who were in danger of starving—you remember how improvident those first colonists were, and how badly their affairs were managed? Once she hid a messenger whom the savages planned to kill; she saved the life of a captured English boy; three times she stole cautiously into Jamestown and warned her new friends of threatened attacks; and she told Smith himself of a trap laid to surprise him, while his party waited for promised provisions.

"Great cheer (corn) will be sent you by and

by," she whispered, "but my father Powhatan and all the power he can make will come afterward, if the braves that bring the corn do not kill you when you are at supper. Hurry away! No, no," she added, refusing a compass he offered her, "I can no take. Indians see it. Powhatan kill me. If know I tell you, I am but dead."

As quietly as she had come through the forest she slipped away, while the Englishmen, ready for the attack, returned in safety to Jamestown.

In the autumn of 1609, tired of the endless quarreling and dissension in the colony, and sorely wounded by an explosion of gunpowder, Smith went back to England. Then Pocahontas made no more visits to Jamestown. Finally word came that Smith was dead and the little Indian girl grieved deeply. After this all friendship between the red men and the whites ceased. The .settlers were often greedy and selfish, frequently breaking their promises to the Indians who soon came to distrust, then to fear and at last to hate them.

A British soldier, Captain Argall, half pirate and half trader, thought of a fine plan to per-

Three times Pocahontas stole cautiously into Jamestown **and** warned her new friends of threatened attacks.

suade Powhatan, who was trying to starve the British out, to keep the peace. This was to get Pocahontas into their power, and the old chief would do anything to ransom her. Now the maid was visiting old Chief Japazaws and his wife on the Potomac River. And so Captain Argall won them to his scheme by promising them a wonderful copper kettle if they succeeded, and threatening them if they failed. The squaw was to bring Pocahontas aboard his ship, lying at anchor in the Potomac.

As they walked along the river bank the old woman said she had seen the English ships three times before, with their great sails like white wings, but she had never been aboard, and oh! how much she wanted to go! Wouldn't her husband take her?

"No, no," he said sternly.

And when she continued to beg, he threatened to beat her—all part of the plan! Pocahontas with her tender heart was moved to pity and offered to go with her, if Japazaws would consent, which he did but only on condition that he accompany them. So the three of them paddled out to the ship, where they were well entertained and invited to a merry supper; after which the Indians with the precious kettle went ashore while Pocahontas was kept a prisoner.

A message was sent to Powhatan that his delight and his darling, Pocahontas, was a captive there at Jamestown and would only be released if he sent back all the Englishmen he held, all the tools and guns and swords he had taken or stolen, and a large amount of corn as a ransom. The maid had a long wait, for the chief made no reply for three months, torn between affection for his daughter and desire for the weapons; and then he sent back only seven Englishmen and a few guns. So the crafty Argall continued to hold her prisoner.

Perhaps she liked the little town better than the smoky long house of her tribe, for she was treated with the greatest friendliness. From the very first she had been warm and cordial to the strangers. Now, an innocent, interesting prisoner, she was honored and petted. Pocahontas had grown to be a woman and had learned the ways of English people. One of the settlers,

POCAHONTAS

Master John Rolfe, who is described in the old records as "an honest and discreet gentleman of good behaviour," fell in love with her, for she was gentle and generous, pretty and graceful, altogether captivating—and she loved him in return.

Rolfe consulted Governor Dale about this marriage and gained his approval. Powhatan also consented and sent his brother to give the bride away, and his two sons and several chiefs of the tribe to be present at the wedding.

In the little church at Jamestown, Pocahontas was baptized and christened Rebecca. And early in April, 1614, she and John Rolfe were married there. The whole colony went to the ceremony, for everybody was interested in the little hostage, and hoped great things from this union—peace with the tribes of red men, and plenty of trade—with Pocahontas as the bond to cement their friendship. They must all have rejoiced when a year later her little son was born, and felt saddened when the family moved out to Bermuda Hundred, a new plantation on the James River where Rolfe raised the first tobacco in Virginia.

Here her husband and Governor Dale and the local minister devoted themselves to teaching her English and the Christian religion. She was eager to learn, for she liked civilized life, though the English customs were in great contrast to the Indian ways. In a short time Pocahontas became so well educated that she had no desire to return to her father. Then she had the greatest affection for her husband, and she dearly loved her son.

When they had been married two years they started to England—Governor Dale, Pocahontas and Rolfe, the baby Thomas, and an old Indian named Tomocomo, whom Powhatan sent as a special guard for his daughter. If life in the colony seemed strange to the forest maid, what must this voyage have been? The great extent of the sea, the many ships, were a marvel to her. At Plymouth the governor of the town came to the wharf to bid her welcome to England. Her journey to London was almost a royal progress.

Everywhere she was received with great honor, as a foreign princess. She was entertained at banquets and receptions. She went to the theaters. She was present at *Twelfth Night* when

POCAHONTAS

Ben Jonson's masque was played; with Lady Delaware she was presented to the king and queen, who welcomed her with pomp and ceremony. She carried herself as though she were the daughter of a king, and among all the ladies of the court none was a greater favorite, for her dark beauty and gentle modest ways won all hearts.

The greatest excitement followed the travelers. Everybody was curious to see Pocahontas. Bishops and great lords and ladies drove in their coaches to call upon her. And in compliment to this princess from the new world many inns and taverns were called "La Belle Sauvage," a name you will still find on old swinging signs in London Town.

The shrewd old chief, Tomocomo, with his tawny skin and shining black hair, dressed in his war feathers and Indian robes, attracted almost as much attention. Powhatan had told him to count the men he saw in England, that the tribe might know the strength of their friends—or enemies? He had given Tomocomo a bundle of sticks whereon he should make a notch for each man he saw.

Long before the party reached London every stick was notched closely, and with an Indian grunt of disgust which meant "My arithmetic fails me!" Tomocomo gave it up and threw away his sticks.

John Smith had again been adventuring and exploring but now, returning to England, he heard every one talking of Pocahontas. Remembering old times and all he owed his little friend, he at once went to visit her. When Smith appeared she was greatly moved and for a long time could not speak. At last she said, "They told me you were dead!"

She reproached him for calling her the formal "Lady Rebecca" and asked why he didn't call her his child, as he used to do?

"But," said Smith, "the king has commanded that you be treated as a princess!"

Pocahontas, as before, had her way, and the two good friends sat down for a long talk of the old days in Virginia, and all that had happened since their separation.

Though she was so petted in England Pocahontas did not really belong there. More and more her thoughts turned toward home. She wearied of crowded London and longed for the forest again. Every day she would stand by the window, looking toward the west where Virginia and her early life lay. She thought much of the old days, of the changes that had come to her and to her people, with the appearance of the fair-haired stranger and his Englishmen. Rolfe grew alarmed at her evident home-sickness, and feared she would fall ill with longing. But they must wait till the ship at Gravesend took on her supplies for the long trip to America, and was loaded with the many cases being sent to Virginia.

At last, word came that all was ready and sailors were sent to take them aboard. But though she had set her face to the west, Pocahontas was not to return to America. A sudden weakness overcame her, gently she fell asleep, and at twenty-two in a foreign land, she died and was buried in the little church at Gravesend.

Her son Thomas was educated in England by his uncle, a London merchant. But when he was grown he returned to Virginia, and among his descendants were many families of that state, proud to claim as their ancestor the tomboy Pocahontas. One of them was William Henry Harrison, president of the United States; another John Randolph, of Roanoke, a man famous in his day, for many years a member of Congress in House and Senate. When he rose to speak there, his flashing black eyes and jet-black hair, his brown parchment-like face seamed with a thousand small wrinkles, his lean figure, with long arms and long bony forefinger, his bursts of brilliant oratory, would remind people of his forebears, and they would say, "Yes, Randolph boasts of the blood of Pocahontas in his veins." Years later, in our own century, another descendant, Edith Bolling Wilson, became mistress of the White House, the first lady in the land.

Pocahontas is the first woman who made history in our country. Her story is full of romance, of adventure, of gentleness and daring courage. Far more she did than save Smith's life; for it was through her friendship with the English that the colony was supplied with food. It was her marriage that made possible, as long as Powhatan

POCAHONTAS

lived, peace between the two peoples. It was she, said John Smith, who saved Virginia from famine, confusion and death.

CHAPTER II

ANNE HUTCHINSON

1590-1643

ANNE MARBURY was an English girl who lived in Lincolnshire, near the town of Boston. Her father was a Puritan minister, preaching there and in London. In Lincolnshire Anne passed her girlhood, doubtless hearing a great deal of theological controversy and religious discussion, for this was the time of the Puritan revolt in England, and of great religious excitement. Naturally intelligent and earnest, her mental powers were aroused and quickened.

At an early age she married William Hutchinson, "a very honest and peaceable man of good estate." And in 1634 with her husband and children she journeyed to America—the outcome of the Reverend John Cotton's leaving England because of his persecution by the bishops. Anne Hutchinson had been one of his most ardent disciples in the church at old Boston, and was now to sit under him in the new Boston.

ANNE HUTCHINSON

It was a pleasant voyage of seven weeks, in the good ship *Griffen*. There were over a hundred passengers, among them two ministers, so you may be sure there were sermons and prayers and religious discussions all during the crossing. Indeed Mistress Anne Hutchinson was so outspoken in her doctrines that, when they landed, one of these ministers reported her to the governor as holding dangerous beliefs. Though her husband was accepted at once, the colony leaders took a week's time to look into her liberal views, and then examined her rigorously before admitting her to membership in the church.

For Massachusetts, you remember, was settled by Puritans who had met persecution in England, and had braved the dangers of the long voyage and the greater dangers of hunger and illness in a new land, in order to worship God in their own way. In accomplishing this they became as intolerant as those from whom they had fled. Indeed there was a far closer relation of church and state in Massachusetts than in England. The only liberty the fathers allowed was the liberty to believe just as they believed. They were right, others were wrong, and on this theory they regulated everything, both religious and civil.

Until their own house could be built, Mistress Anne Hutchinson and some of the children lived at the Reverend Cotton's; and for the three years the family remained in Boston, their home was across the street from John Winthrop's. Almost immediately this house became the social center of the town and Anne Hutchinson had a leading place among the three hundred inhabitants and the fast friendship of the brilliant young Englishman, Sir Harry Vane, then serving a term as governor of the colony. The women loved her for her goodness of heart, her cheerful neighborliness, her great skill in nursing. Both men and women welcomed her intellectual and magnetic personality. She had a vigorous mind, a dauntless courage, a natural gift for leadership; she was capable, energetic, amiable.

And there was another reason why the women liked her. The colonists had two church services on Sunday, with sermons sometimes three hours long; Thursday lectures, and a Saturday night meeting. There was also during the week religious discussion for the men. Mrs. Hutchinson started meetings for women—a new departure, for never before had women met for independent thought and action. At first this won high approval. The women—forty, sixty, sometimes eighty of them, even a hundred, for they came from near-by towns as well as from Boston homes—were soon holding regular meetings to review the sermons of the Sunday before, with Mistress Anne's comment and interpretation.

"All the faithful embraced her conference," a contemporary record describes the gatherings, "and blessed God for her fruitful discourses."

But from a review of the sermons to discussion and criticism of them and the ministers as well was a short step. It soon began to be said that Anne Hutchinson cast reproaches on those who preached "a covenant by works" instead of the "covenant by grace" in which she fervently believed. Such freedom of speech could not be tolerated by the good Puritans, and a theological dispute arose which threatened the very life of the colony. There were two parties, grace and works. Politics became a matter of Hutchinson opinions, for political lines and religious lines coincided exactly. Indeed there was no separation of church and state; the leaders of one controlled the policy of the other.

From the beginning of the colony the preachers had had an unlimited influence. Now they complained that "more resort to Mrs. Hutchinson for council about matters of conscience than to any minister in the country." Moreover this grace and works difficulty was carried into every phase of life. Some people turned their backs contemptuously and walked out of meeting when a preacher not under a covenant of grace entered the pulpit. Others interrupted the services with questions of controversy. Indeed it was carried so far that when the Pequot Indians became aggressive and dangerous and it was necessary to send troops against them, the Boston soldiers refused to be mustered into service, because the chaplain, drawn by lot, preached a covenant of works, and they disagreed with his Sunday sermon! The whole town of Boston, the whole colony of Massachusetts, church and state, were set in commotion and turmoil. This theological quarrel was a stumbling block in the way of all progress.

The ministers so freely criticized were embittered and determined to call Mistress Hutchinson and her doctrines to account. So they summoned a synod, all the clergymen and magistrates of Massachusetts, who met in Cambridge for full three weeks, discussing some eighty-two opinions which they condemned—some as dangerous, some blasphemous, some erroneous, and all unsafe. The women's meetings were forbidden as "disorderly and without rule."

Forbidden to speak in public Anne Hutchinson continued to hold meetings in her own house. Roger Williams, who was shortly to feel the full displeasure of the Puritan leaders, said that in view of her usefulness as a nurse and a neighbor, she ought to be allowed to speak when she chose and to say what she wished, "because if it be a lie, it will die of itself; and if it be truth, we ought to know it."

The authorities in Massachusetts were in constant dread of losing their charter, which was especially endangered by reports of disorderly proceedings. And certainly nothing had provoked so much disorder and sedition as the course taken by Mistress Anne. Both politically and religiously they felt it a duty to suppress her party. So in October, 1637, she was brought to trial before the General Court of Massachusetts, sitting in the meeting-house in Cambridge.

"Mrs. Hutchinson," said Winthrop, presiding, "you are called here as one of those that have troubled the peace of the commonwealth and the churches here. . . . You have maintained a meeting and an assembly in your house that hath been condemned by the general assembly as a thing not tolerable nor comely in the sight of God nor fitting for your sex, and notwithstanding that was cried down you have continued the same. Therefore we have thought good to send for you to understand how things are, that if you be in an erroneous way we may reduce you that so you may become a profitable member here among us, otherwise if you be obstinate in your course that then the court may take such course that you may trouble us no further."

This trial was at once a civil, judicial and ecclesiastical process, lasting through two long weary days. Extremely tiring and exhausting must have been the examination, for the deputy-governor complained that they would all be sick from fasting! The forty-three men who tried her were like an English court of High Commission, almost like the Inquisition. For Anne Hutchinson had no lawyer. They even kept her standing until she almost fell from fatigue, before they allowed her to answer seated.

Governor and deputy, magistrates and judges were arrayed against her. They examined and cross-examined her. They badgered and insulted and sneered at her. They browbeat and silenced her witnesses, in absolute disregard of fair play. Only one man of them all defended her, saying with spirit, "There is no law of God that she has broken, nor any law of the country, and she deserves no censure."

They found it no easy thing to make her trap herself. Their fine theological distinctions were familiar ground to her. She had a ready grasp of scriptural authority, and wonderful skill in using her intellectual power to prove her spiritual position. With the ability and clearness of a trained advocate she conducted her case, showing tact and judgment and self-reliance, and always with the demeanor of a lady. What Winthrop described as her "nimble wit and voluble tongue" never deserted her, though she was hard pressed by the keenest minds of the colony.

When they failed to prove her women's meetings opposed to the Bible, they fell back on the argument of their authority and said, "We are your judges, and not you ours, and we must compel you to it."

When she answered to some of their questions, "That s matter of conscience, sir," stern Governor Winthrop replied, "Your conscience you must keep, or it must be kept for you."

It was the deputy-governor who summed the whole matter up:

"About three years ago we were all in peace. Mrs. Hutchinson from that time she came hath made a disturbance. . . . She hath vented divers of her strange opinions and hath made parties. . . . She in particular hath disparaged all our ministers. . . . Why this is not to be suffered, and therefore being driven to the foundation and it being found that Mrs. Hutchinson . . . hath been the cause of what is fallen out, why we must take away the foundation and the building will fall."

ANNE HUTCHINSON

The result of the trial might have been announced before it opened. Read how the court record finishes:

"Governor Winthrop: The Court hath already declared itself satisfied concerning the things you hear, and concerning the troublesomeness of her spirit, and the danger of her course amongst us, which is not to be suffered. Therefore if it be the mind of the Court that Mrs. Hutchinson, for these things that appear before us, is unfit for our society, and if it be the mind of the Court that she shall be banished out of our liberties, and imprisoned till she be sent away, let them hold up their hands."

All but three held up their hands.

"Governor Winthrop: Mrs. Hutchinson, you hear the sentence of the Court. It is that you are banished from out our jurisdiction as being a woman not fit for our society, and you are to be imprisoned till the Court send you away.

"Mrs. Hutchinson: I desire to know wherefore I am banished.

"Governor Winthrop: Say no more. The Court knows wherefore, and is satisfied."

Semi-imprisonment Mistress Anne had all that winter, in the house of a man in Roxbury whose brother was one of her most bitter enemies. She was sent up to Boston to be admonished by the elders of the church; and when she refused to sign an absolute retraction of her opinions, and would not promise to hold any more meetings, she was excommunicated.

The sentence of banishment was carried out in March of 1638. To the sorrow of many of the colonists, William Hutchinson went with his wife. He refused their invitations to remain, saying, "For I am more dearly tied to my wife than to the church. . . . And I do think her a saint and servant of God." With husband and children and seventy friends Mistress Anne went to Rhode Island where Roger Williams offered the party a friendly refuge. From the Indians they bought an island, for ten coats, twenty hoes, and forty fathoms of white wampum; and lived there until 1642 when William Hutchinson died.

Hearing a rumor that Massachusetts was trying to extend her control over Rhode Island, the settlers left for a new site in the Dutch colony to the west. A year later a friendly Indian one morning visited Anne Hutchinson's house. Seeing that the family was defenseless he returned that night

came over to America as ballast in one of William Penn's vessels. It is still standing, in a good state of preservation, and very little changed from the old days, with its wide doors, big cupboards, narrow stairs and tiny window-panes. The front room was the shop, where Elizabeth and John waited on customers; and next to this was the back parlor.

Now Elizabeth Ross was not only an energetic and trained upholsterer, she was also the most skilful needlewoman in Philadelphia, and had a great reputation for embroidering and darning. There was a story current of a young lady visiting in the city, who wanted an elaborately embroidered frock mended. She was directed to take it to Mistress Betsy Ross. And the owner said, when it was finished, that the darning was the handsomest part of the gown! Considerable artistic skill had Betsy, too, for she could draw free-hand, very rapidly and accurately, the complicated designs used in those days for quilting. Withal she was a thoroughly efficient housekeeper.

The happiness of the Ross family was not to last long. The spirit of liberty was awakening among the colonists, the spirit of resistance to the demands of the mother country. In common with many patriotic women, Betsy Ross saw her husband march away for military service. With several other young men he was guarding cannon balls and artillery stores on one of the city wharves along the Delaware River, when he received a serious injury, from the effects of which he died in January, 1776, after long and anxious nursing on the part of his young wife. He was buried in the Christ Church burying-ground; and in that historic old Philadelphia church you can still see the Ross pew, marked with the Stars and Stripes.

There was Betsy Ross, a widow at twenty-four. She determined to maintain herself independently, if possible, and to continue alone the upholstery business they had developed together. About five months after her husband's death, some time between the twenty-second of May and the fifth of June, she was one day working in the shop when three gentlemen called.

The first was General Washington, in Philadelphia for a few days to consult the Continental

Congress. Mistress Ross had frequently seen him, for the story is that he had visited her shop more than once, to have her embroider the ruffles for his shirts, an important branch of fine hand-sewing in those days. With him was Robert Morris, to go down in history as the treasurer and financier of the Revolution; and her husband's uncle, Colonel George Ross, a signer of the Declaration of Independence.

These gentlemen had come to consult her. She knew, of course, how the various banners carried by troops from the different colonies, as well as by different regiments, had caused confusion and might mean danger. It was time to do away with the pine tree flag, the beaver flag, the rattlesnake flag, the hope flag, the silver crescent flag, the anchor flag, the liberty tree flag, and all the rest of them, and have a single standard for the American army. Betsy Ross had heard, too, of the Cambridge flag, often called the grand union flag, which Washington had raised the New Year's day before, a flag half English, half American, with thirteen red and white stripes, and the crosses of St. George and St. Andrew. But since the first of the year events had moved rapidly and the desire for separation from England had become steadily stronger. A new flag was needed, to show the growing spirit of Americanism—which was soon to crystallize on the fourth of July.

All this Betsy Ross knew, as a good patriot would. And she could not have been greatly surprised when General Washington said they had come to consult her about a national flag.

"Can you make a flag?" he asked.

Modestly and with some diffidence she replied, "I don't know, sir, but I can try."

Then in the little back parlor Washington showed her a rough sketch he had made—a square flag with thirteen stripes of red and white, and thirteen stars in the blue canton. He asked her opinion of the design. With unerring accuracy of eye she saw at once what was needed to make the flag more beautiful, more attractive. She suggested that the proportions be changed, so that the length would be a third more than the width; that the thirteen stars should not be scattered irregularly over the canton, but grouped to form some design, say a circle or a star, or placed in parallel rows; and lastly that a five-pointed star was more symmetrical than one with six points.

"But," asked Washington, "isn't it more difficult to make?"

In answer practical Betsy Ross took up a piece of paper, folded it over, and with one clip of her scissors cleverly made a perfect star with five even points.

That was sufficient, and the general drew up his chair to her table and made another pencil sketch, embodying her three suggestions. The second sketch was copied and colored by a Philadelphia artist, William Barrett, a painter of some note, who returned it to Mistress Ross. Meantime not knowing just how to make a flag, for it must be sewed in a particular way, she went to a shipping merchant, an old Scotchman who was a friend of Robert Morris, to borrow a ship's flag as a guide.

And in this way Betsy Ross made the first Stars and Stripes. To try the effect, the new flag was run up to the peak of one of the vessels in the Delaware River, the story goes, a ship commanded by Paul Jones; and the result was so pleasing that on the same day the flag was carried into Congress and approved. At the same time the Congress passed a resolution putting Paul Jones in command of the *Ranger*.

"The flag and I were born the same day and hour," Jones used to say. "We are twins, we can not be parted in life or death. So long as we can float, we shall float together. If we must sink we shall go down as one."

It was not until June 14, 1777, that the Continental Congress passed a resolution formally adopting this flag as the national standard, a resolution reported to have been introduced by John Adams. Another and unexplained delay followed, for not until September was this resolution publicly promulgated.

The fact that Betsy Ross was not named in the *Congressional Record* has been considered by some sufficient evidence that the whole story is a myth. But there is no Congressional record whatever about the Cambridge flag, which was used for almost a year. Is it surprising then that its modification was not put on record promptly? There was no newspaper notice of the

resolution of June fourteenth, the basis of our
modern flag day. And in all the letters and
diaries and writings of the time, there is found
no mention of this flag resolution. Betsy Ross
had made the flag months earlier, and all that
time it had been gradually coming into use. Does
not that explain the apparent lack of interest?
This story she told, over and over and over,
to her daughters and grandchildren, and in later
years they wrote the account down, just as they
had heard it from her, and as you have read it
here.

We know too from other records that before
the flag was officially adopted by Congress, Elizabeth Ross was engaged in flagmaking. For in
May of 1777 the state navy board of Pennsylvania
passed an order to pay her the sum of fourteen
pounds, twelve shillings and two pence, for making ships' colors for the fleet in the Delaware
River. And immediately after the resolution did
pass, she was authorized to proceed at once to
manufacture a large number of flags for the Continental Congress.

For more than fifty years Betsy Ross continued

to make government flags, with her daughters and nieces, and later her grandchildren, helping her. She continued to sew red and white stripes together and put five-pointed stars on the blue canton, even after her second marriage to a sea captain, while he went back and forth to Europe on his dangerous business, and during his imprisonment in England, where he died. When his friend, who had been a fellow-prisoner, was finally released and returned to Philadelphia to deliver to Betsy Ross her husband's little property, she married this messenger and kept on making flags. Except for a brief residence with her daughter, she continued to live in the quaint little house on Arch Street where the flag was born. Shortly before her death she became completely blind; but her busy fingers must keep on stitching, and with her little grandsons to sort the colors for her, she sewed happily on carpet rags.

When Mistress Ross retired from the business of making flags her daughter Clarissa took over this work and carried it on until 1857. Flags of many kinds they made—for army and navy, for arsenals and the merchant marine; flags with thirteen stars in a circle, like a round-robin to show that one state should have no precedence over the others; flags with stars in parallel rows of four, five and four; flags with fifteen stripes and stars; flags bearing the arms of Pennsylvania, painted on the silk by William Barrett.

It was George Washington, more than any other, who seems to have been most interested in the question of a national flag. But it was to the skilled needlewoman that he took his first rough design, to have her opinion of its worth. It is to Betsy Ross that much of the beauty of our flag is due. A true patriot of Revolutionary times, her humble life is an incentive to others, showing that there is more than one way to serve the nation—even if one is known only as a maker of ruffles.

CHAPTER IV

MARY LINDLEY MURRAY

1720-1782

EXCEPT for one day's events the story of Mrs. Murray is quickly told. A famous Quaker belle in Philadelphia was the beautiful Mary Lindley. After her marriage to Robert Murray, a merchant, she lived near Lancaster, Pennsylvania, and in North Carolina, until in 1753 they moved to New York City, where Murray and Sansom soon became one of the great merchandising firms of the time. There were a dozen children in the Murray household, one son being Lindley Murray, the grammarian. Hoping the milder climate would benefit her husband's health, Mrs. Murray took her family to England where they lived for eleven years, returning to America during the first year of the Revolution.

Always a belle, she is described as a lady of great dignity and stateliness of manner, mild and amiable, quick at repartee. She and her daughters were ardent patriots, but Mr. Murray, the rich merchant and landowner, was not unnaturally a Tory, loyal to the Crown. Shortly before peace was made with England, after the success at Yorktown had crowned Washington's efforts for America, Mrs. Murray died.

But on the fifteenth of September, 1776, Mary Lindley Murray gave aid to Washington, her contribution to the War for Independence being woman's wit and beauty. That September was a difficult month for the patriots. At the end of August had come the British victory at the battle of Long Island, and Washington's skilful retreat to Manhattan. As usual Howe was dilatory in following and not until sixteen days later did he cross with his troops.

The fifteenth of September was a hot day. From their country house on a hill near the center of Manhattan Island the Murrays looked down on the new breastworks thrown up at Kip's Bay. They knew the Americans were scattered—the main force at the north on Harlem Heights, and Putnam's men far to the south. Then up the East River sailed five British men-of-war and anchored opposite the Murray house, in the bay.

Before the handful of militiamen had time to wonder why the ships had come, out swarmed a number of dories. To the Murrays, watching from the hill half a mile away, the river seemed suddenly dyed scarlet, for under cover of the warships' guns eighty-four boats landed the British soldiers, while up the bank clambered four thousand Redcoats, driving the Americans before them. At the first fire, the Continentals fled from their trenches back to higher ground, fled in headlong retreat.

Four miles to the north Washington heard the booming of cannon and galloped down to the scene of action. To his astonishment and consternation his men were flying in all directions. Riding excitedly into the midst of the runaways he shouted, "Take to the wall! Take to the cornfield!" His attempt to rally them was vain. Chagrined he would have ridden straight into danger, had not an aide seized his horse's bridle and turned the general back toward safety. In great confusion and disorder the post at the bay was deserted. And there were Putnam's divisions to the south, separated from the main army, caught in a trap if the British threw their men across the island.

Now this was exactly General Howe's plan, but he failed to count Mrs. Murray into his scheme. From the bay he marched west for a half-mile until he came to the Murray house. Set in a wide lawn, with extensive gardens on either side, "Belmont" was considered one of the loveliest spots on the island. Its fair mistress had heard the firing, had seen the disorderly retreat and realized what the Americans needed most of all was time. She would make it for them!

She posted a maid in the cupola of the great square mansion, with orders to report to her by signals how Putnam was progressing. It was a season of extreme drought, and the dense clouds of dust made it easy to follow his march. At the proper time Mrs. Murray sent a negro servant with a cordial invitation to General Howe and his staff to dine with her. This genial Quaker lady was not unknown to the Britishers, for they had met her in England. Here was an opportunity to renew the acquaintance of peaceful days, but duty first, for a general.

"I do thank you, madam," was Howe's cour-
teous reply, "but I must first catch that rascally
Yankee, Putnam."

"Did thee not hear he had gone?" was her quick
rejoinder. "It is too late to catch him. Pursuit
is hopeless. Thee had better come in and dine."

If Putnam was really out of reach there was
no need for haste, and the day was sweltering.
So across the broad veranda and into the cool
attractive house went Howe, with Clinton and
Cornwallis and Governor Tryon, and others of
his staff. Outside, in the hot September sun, his
men rested and prepared and ate their midday
meal. Within, Mrs. Murray and her beautiful
daughters proved charming hostesses, with a
warm welcome for their English guests. The
good merchant, who was known to be heartily
loyal to the king, was not at home that day, but
his rare old Madeira was served with dainty cakes
after the dinner.

So witty and delightful was the talk, so keenly
did the others enjoy Tryon's raillery of their
hostess about her patriot friends and how the
ragged Continentals had run that morning, that

not one of them noticed the rapid flight of time.
And you may be sure that Mistress Murray pro-
longed their stay, bearing the teasing with rare
good humor and making herself thoroughly agree-
able, for every moment gained would count.

Meanwhile, half a mile to the west, Putnam was
hurrying northward, his march greatly ham-
pered by his cannon, his camp impedimenta, and
the refugee women and children. Terribly they
suffered from the heat. Alexander Hamilton gal-
lantly led one company. A young major, Aaron
Burr, acted as guide, for he knew every foot of
the ground; riding back and forth he showed the
patriots bypaths and lanes through the thickets,
until ahead they saw Washington's tents on the
heights of Harlem, and knew they were safe.
Through Mrs. Murray's hospitality the British
had lost their chance to take four thousand prisoners. Her own wit and her husband's wine had
saved the day.

Behind the Harlem entrenchments the patriots
were ready for Howe's attack the following morning, and a spirited encounter that was in the buck-
wheat field. But the British failed to capture the

heights and so force Washington off the island. Counted only by the number of men engaged, this was really not a great battle, but it was a great victory for the Americans who had lost heart after their defeat on Long Island and their forced evacuation of New York. It restored their confidence and put new hope into their hearts. It clinched Washington's determination and made possible the brilliant exploits at Trenton and Princeton.

In Revolutionary journals kept by American and British soldiers you will find Howe's delay at the Murray home given as the reason for Putnam's escape. And it was a common saying among the Americans that the beautiful Quaker lady had saved "Old Put," the wolf-killer, and his four thousand men. For patriotism and courage do not exist only behind a bayonet. One can be heroic in any way that conquers circumstances.

CHAPTER V

MOLLY PITCHER

1754-1832

MARY LUDWIG, the daughter of a German settler, was born on a small farm between Princeton and Trenton in New Jersey. Her father was a dairyman and Molly, like other children of her parentage, was brought up to work hard. A typical German peasant girl, heavy-set, strong and sturdy, she toiled in the fields, she milked the cows, and drove them to pasture. The story is that she could swing a three-bushel sack of wheat to her shoulder and carry it to the upstairs room of the granary; and this strength and endurance stood her in good stead years later, for after the battle of Princeton she picked up a wounded soldier, carried him two miles to a farmhouse, and there nursed him back to health.

A Mrs. Irvine from Carlisle, visiting in Trenton, wished to take a young girl home with her to help in the housework. She saw buxom Molly Ludwig, liked her honest face and wholesome, energetic appearance, and on her return took the German girl with her. For some years Molly lived with Doctor and Mrs. Irvine, and proved to be a valuable assistant in their home. She did not like sewing, but she was expert at scrubbing and scouring and washing—any kind of violent exercise!

Near the Irvines' house was a little barber shop kept by an Irishman, John Hays. Whenever Molly was scrubbing the front steps or scouring the door-knocker, the young barber was sure to be watching from his window. When the girl was about sixteen years old, this courting ended in marriage.

Then suddenly Carlisle heard the news of Lexington, nothing but war was talked of. Doctor Irvine, who had served in the French and Indian campaigns, was colonel of a Pennsylvania regiment. Hays went as gunner in the artillery, and when his time was out reenlisted under Colonel Irvine.

"I'm proud to be a soldier's wife," was Molly's answer when he told her he must go. "I'll stand by you!" But neither of them guessed that this would literally come true. No slacker, she waved him a cheerful good-by, and went on with her household duties for Mrs. Irvine. But when a few months later Hays sent her word to go back to her father's, as the troops were encamped near by and he could see her occasionally, she too said, "I must go," and rode off behind the messenger. At home again Molly donned her rough farm garments, helping with the cattle, working in the fields as before. And frequently John Hays paid a flying visit to the little farm, and Molly occasionally went to visit him in camp.

During the Revolution it was not unusual for wives to accompany their soldier husbands, not to fight, but to wash and mend and cook, to care for the sick and wounded. Once while Molly was cooking for the men, she had a large kettle over the fire which she wanted to remove, so she called to a passing soldier to help her. His prompt compliance and kindness of manner made her ask his name, and she was so astonished that she almost dropped the kettle when she heard his reply, "I am General Washington."

Hays and Doctor Irvine were both soldiers.

49

Molly's heart was with them and with the country, fighting for independence. All she needed was the opportunity to show of what mettle she was made. This came at the battle of Monmouth Court House.

After the winter's drilling at Valley Forge, Washington followed closely behind Clinton, who was marching across New Jersey from Philadelphia. The British had an enormous amount of baggage and their line was twenty miles long. The Americans waited for the chance to attack. Cornwallis brought his men into line of action opposite Lee, who ordered a retreat. Washington's angry rebuke to Lee, plus the splendid work of Mad Anthony Wayne and Lafayette and Knox and Greene, saved the day for the patriot army. Lee's record was stained by this traitorous action. The outstanding hero of the day was Molly Hays.

It was a very hot June Sunday. The blazing sun beat down on both armies with scorching, record-breaking heat. Men and horses were well-nigh overcome. The Americans, however, had the advantage, for they were dressed for summer weather and had left their packs by the meeting-house at Freehold. The British had heavy woolen uniforms and full knapsacks. The Hessians carried in addition to all this the load of decorations which Frederick the Great thought necessary for his soldiers.

The air was sultry. Not a leaf stirred on the maple trees. Men dropped fainting to the earth, from sunstroke. Yet the American guns were fired vigorously, sending their shot across the swamp into the British ranks, and until night the battle went on. Sometimes under shelter, sometimes under fire, Molly Hays went back and forth to the spring, carrying water for the suffering men, and for wetting the sponges to swab out the cannon. And the weary thirsty soldiers, welcoming the sight of her with the sparkling water, would call out gratefully, "Here comes Molly with her pitcher!" a call soon shortened to "Molly Pitcher!"

On one of her trips from the well Molly saw her husband fall suddenly. Accounts differ as to whether he was wounded, or had a sunstroke working in the blistering heat near the cannon. General Knox, in charge of the battery, had no competent man to put in Hays' place and was about to withdraw the gun, when Molly sprang forward, seized the rammer and fired. A moment was sufficient to show that she could fill her husband's position, that she had the strength and nerve for his task. The men cheered as she loaded and fired shot after shot, with the skill of a veteran gunner. Her hair disheveled, her eyes blazing, her hot face begrimed with powder and smoke and dust, barefooted like many of the soldiers, she kept on with her perilous work. That night the British stole silently away, leaving their dead and wounded, with Washington in possession of the field. This victory was the last battle of importance in the North, the beginning of a brighter period for the Americans.

The story of Molly Pitcher's brave act spread through the camp. General Greene thanked her, "in the name of the army." The next morning in her dusty, torn, powder-stained dress, she was presented to Washington. With such honor as he would have shown to one of his gallant men, he spoke a few words of sympathy and praise, gave her a sergeant's commission, and later placed her name on the list of half-pay officers for life.

An old Revolutionary rhyme tells the story:

"Moll Pitcher she stood by her gun
And rammed the charges home, sir;
And thus on Monmouth's bloody field
A sergeant did become, sir."

Hays was the proudest man in the army, at Washington's praise of his wife, when he heard the soldiers cheer her to the echo. Lafayette asked if his men "might have the pleasure of giving Madame a trifle," and invited Molly to review his troops. Between two long lines of French officers she passed, and at the end her hat was filled with gold crowns.

Until the close of the Revolution, Molly Hays, or Molly Pitcher, as she was always called, remained with the army; and following her husband's death, shortly after the war ended, she lived for many years at the Carlisle barracks, cooking and washing for the soldiers. In 1794 she saw General Washington again, for when he was traveling through Pennsylvania, he stopped near Carlisle, and Molly Pitcher made a pil-

grimage on foot to see him. When her story
was recalled to the general he greeted her most
cordially.

In 1822 the legislature of Pennsylvania, without a dissenting voice, voted her the sum of forty
dollars, and an annuity of that amount during her
lifetime. When she died ten years later, she was
buried with military honors, a company of soldiers firing a salute. On the Fourth of July, 1876,
there was unveiled at her grave a white marble
monument inscribed to "Molly Pitcher, the heroine of Monmouth." And each year on the thirtieth
of May, along with the score of Revolutionary
graves in the churchyard, hers is decorated with
flowers by the people of Carlisle.

In the little park at Freehold a monument was
erected to commemorate the victory of Monmouth
Court House, and on one of its five panels Molly
Pitcher is shown, barefooted, ramming home the
charge, her husband lying exhausted at her feet.
She was a real heroine, when the need came, a
true and courageous soldier.

CHAPTER VI

MARTHA WASHINGTON

1732-1802

ON a great Virginia plantation in the year
1732 Martha Dandridge was born. Her
father was a prominent landowner and his daughter had the usual education of the time—not much
schooling in comparison with to-day, but she
learned to play the spinet, to dance gracefully, and
to sew with all the mysteries of elaborate stitches.
A well-behaved, pretty child she was who at fifteen made her début in Williamsburg, the capital
of Virginia, which then afforded the gayest social
life in America. Dressed in a stiff bodice and
flowered petticoat, Martha was the belle of the
ball, and of many succeeding ones as well, for at
once she became a great favorite.

When she was barely eighteen she married
Daniel Parke Custis, a wealthy landowner, who
was more than twenty years her senior. They
lived near Williamsburg at his country home, the

55

"White House." Seven years later he died, leaving her with two young children and a great fortune—thousands of pounds and thousands of acres of Virginia land.

In May, 1758, Mrs. Custis was visiting at Major Chamberlayne's, when her host brought an unexpected guest—none other than young Colonel George Washington, already a military hero and commander of the Virginia troops. He was en route to Williamsburg to report to the governor on the needs of his regiments, and when Major Chamberlayne pressed him to stop, he had at first refused, but yielded when told that the prettiest and richest widow in all Virginia was there.

He would stay for dinner then, but must go on at once, and gave orders accordingly to his servant, Bishop, bequeathed to him by General Braddock. But when dinner was over and the horses were brought round no Washington appeared, though Bishop had never known his master to be late before. In the drawing-room the young colonel and the young widow were talking, oblivious to everything else, while the impatient steeds pawed the drive restlessly. Till the day was done and twilight at hand Washington loitered.

"No guest can leave my house after sunset," said the major, and insisted that he must stay the night. Late the next morning Bishop and his master rode away to Williamsburg. The little widow in the white dimity frock, with the cluster of May-blossoms at her belt, and the little white cap half covering her soft, wavy brown hair, had completely captivated the soldier. His business in the town completed, he rode on to the "White House."

"Is your mistress at home?" he asked the negro who met him at the ferry.

"Yes, sah," was the reply, and the man added, his white teeth flashing in a broad smile, "I reckon you's the man what's 'spected!"

Evidently he was, for when, on the following day, Washington left for camp and the western campaign against Fort Duquesne, the two were engaged.

In January, 1759, when they had met just four times, Mrs. Custis and George Washington were married. A brilliant scene the wedding was. The guests included wealthy planters and their wives and daughters, all very grand in their satins and brocades, English officers in army and navy uniforms, the governor of Virginia, in scarlet embroidered with gold, with a bag wig. The groom wore a blue suit, the coat lined with scarlet silk and trimmed with silver, an embroidered white satin waistcoat, with knee and shoe buckles of gold; while in contrast to his six feet two was the little bride in a petticoat of white quilted satin, with an overdress of white corded silk interwoven with silver threads, high-heeled satin shoes with diamond buckles, point lace ruffles and pearls. At the door, attracting almost as much attention as the wedding party, stood Bishop in his red coat, holding his master's chestnut horse.

With her three bridesmaids Mrs. Washington drove to her home in a coach and six, while her husband and a group of his friends rode beside them. Thus began their forty years of married life.

After a few months in Williamsburg, to settle the business of the Custis estate and to attend the meetings of the House of Burgesses, of which

Washington had been elected a member during his campaign against the French, he took his bride to Mount Vernon, his eight-thousand acre plantation on the Potomac River. Here they planned to live quietly, he busy with his fields and flocks, she with the large household, and both enjoying the growth of the Custis children. In a white apron and cap, with a bunch of keys jingling at her side, Mrs. Washington supervised the busy kitchen and slave quarters, looked after the strict training and the lessons of the children, and was a charming hostess to their guests.

But public affairs changed and with them this quiet happy life. The stamp act and oppressive taxes stirred the colonies. Like many patriot women, Martha Washington ceased using tea at her table, ceased to buy English cloth and other goods of English manufacture. No less than sixteen spinning-wheels were kept busy at Mount Vernon, and on the looms homespun was woven for the family's clothing and for the large number of slaves.

Rapidly events moved to a crisis. The first Continental Congress was called, and Washington

elected as one of Virginia's three delegates. When
the party started north Mrs. Washington saw
them off with these words of wifely appreciation,
"I hope you will all stand firm. I know George
will. God be with you, gentlemen."

And this was not idle talk on her part, for she
foresaw plainly the consequences. At the many
discussions and debates which had occurred at
their home, for and against English policy, she
had said little, but had listened intelligently. She
summed it up in writing to a friend:

"Dark days and darker nights, domestic happiness suspended, social enjoyments abandoned,
property put in jeopardy—but what are all these
evils when compared with the fate of which the
Port Bill may be only a threat? My mind is made
up, my heart is in the cause."

The second Congress met the following May
and Washington was unanimously chosen com-
mander-in-chief of the army. He wrote this news
to his wife at Mount Vernon, adding that he
hoped to return in the autumn. Instead he then
invited her to come to him in Cambridge, but carefully pointed out the difficulties of the journey.
Unhesitating, undismayed, a true soldier's wife,

she set out for the long trip to the North, as though it were the most natural thing in the world to leave the ease and security of her southern home and spend the winter in a New England camp on the outskirts of a city held by the enemy.

The coach with its four horses, and postillions in white and scarlet livery, attracted great attention. In the country people rushed to doors and windows to get a sight of her. In the towns she was met by escorts of Continental soldiers, the ringing of bells, and enthusiastic cheering. With a mingled feeling of pride and wonder this little woman, who had never been out of Virginia, realized what it was to be the wife of General Washington.

This was a real farewell to the quiet plantation and the beginning of her public life. Except for the year when Trenton and Princeton and active winter campaigning made it too dangerous for women to be present, it was Martha Washington's custom to join her husband when the army went into winter quarters, and to march back home when work opened with the spring. Thus she heard the first and last gun of every

campaign, and described herself as a perambulator
for those eight years.

Because she was the wife of the general, it did
not follow that she could live in luxury. In Cambridge to be sure headquarters were in the Craigie
House, later the home of the poet Longfellow; and
here Mrs. Washington had some social life, with
the wives of the Harvard professors. But in
other places lodgings were often very, very un-
comfortable, "a squeezed-up room or two." At
Valley Forge a log cabin was built—near a
Quaker farmhouse where the Washingtons had
two rooms—to serve as a kitchen and dining-
room; but when this same plan was proposed for
the headquarters at Morristown, no lumber was
available! At Newburgh their inconvenient dining-room had one window and seven doors, and
the sitting-room was so small that when Washington entertained a French officer, the guest had
to sit on a camp bed.

Martha Washington's presence lessened the
general's cares and broke the monotony of the
long anxious winters. She was always a delightful hostess and even with camp limitations her

hospitality and genial manner reminded her guests of Virginia. Nearly every day some of the young officers and their wives were invited to dinner, the General and Mrs. Washington sitting side by side, while Alexander Hamilton carved.

Martha Washington was always a simple, dignified woman, as a group of Morristown ladies who went to call upon her testified. Having heard that the general's wife was a very grand lady, they wore their best bibs and bands, and most elegant silks and ruffles. Mrs. Washington, in a plain homespun dress and a "specked" (checked) apron, received them very graciously, a half knit stocking in her left hand, the ball of yarn in her pocket. After the usual compliments were over, she resumed her knitting.

"And there we were," described one of the women afterward, "without a stitch of work, and sitting in state, but General Washington's lady was knitting socks!"

She showed them two dresses of cotton and silk, woven at Mount Vernon, the stripes made from ravelings of brown silk stockings and old crimson damask chair covers. She took pains to tell them that the livery of her coachmen was all homespun, save for the scarlet cuffs, made of English material imported long before the war.

After that visit, work for the soldiers, rather than fine feminine clothes, became the fashion in Morristown.

At another New Jersey headquarters Washington was staying at a private house, whose mistress one day saw a coach drive up to the door, with ten dragoons as the escort. Out stepped a plain little woman dressed in brown homespun, wearing a hood; over her bosom was folded a large white kerchief. She must be a maid, thought the hostess, until she saw General Washington greeting her, and inquiring about the children, and his favorite horses at Mount Vernon. The general's wife, dressed like that!

Everywhere the soldiers loved Lady Washington, as they called her. During the sad winter at Valley Forge, when the army was in desperate straits, suffering greatly from lack of food and blankets and clothing, and the consequent constant sickness, she went to share the soldiers' pri-

"And there we were without a stitch of work, and sitting in state,
but General Washington's lady was knitting socks!"

vations and make a spot of cheer in their dreary lives. She arrived in a rough farm sleigh, hired from the innkeeper at the forks of the Brandywine, where the deep snow had forced her to abandon her coach. Stanch patriot that she was, she made light of inconveniences and discomforts and hardships; and never was a woman busier than Martha Washington, all that dismal winter. In a cloak and hood, with her basket on her arm, she went in the deep snow from hut to hut, carrying delicacies for the sick and consolation for the dying, and by her sympathy and generosity stimulating the loyalty and courage of the men. "God bless Lady Washington!" was frequently heard, when her kind, motherly face appeared.

Day after day she assembled in her two rooms the wives of the officers, to knit and patch, and make new garments whenever materials could be secured. No more embroidering and spinet playing, and other light accomplishments! The work these women did at Valley Forge was far-reaching in its effects. News of it spread to Philadelphia, where the British were having a gay winter, and the patriotic ladies there commenced making shirts for the soldiers, and ultimately contributed nearly three thousand garments. Small in amount, perhaps, in comparison with such service to-day; but Martha Washington was a pioneer, anticipating the work of the Sanitary Commission and the American Red Cross.

Officers, soldiers and women, all were steadied by her serenity and unwavering faith. And when the middle of March brought better times, she led in the camp gaiety. The news of the French alliance was celebrated with a grand review. The soldiers cheered for the king of France, for the thirteen states, for their general; then there came shouts of "Long live Lady Washington!" and a thousand hats were tossed into the air in the excitement.

Yorktown and victory, and the end of the war in sight, but Washington must remain on duty until peace was actually signed. Martha Washington was present, sitting in the gallery of the old capitol at Annapolis, when he resigned his commission; and together they drove to Mount Vernon, arriving on Christmas Eve. Standing at the door of his cottage to welcome them was old

Bishop, dressed in the scarlet regimentals he had worn at Braddock's defeat. All the servants and slaves assembled, and such a Christmas celebration as Mount Vernon had!

More than all else the Washingtons longed for quiet days on their plantation, to enjoy the rest they so much needed. But there were guests innumerable, so that Mount Vernon was described as a well-resorted tavern. When he had been home almost two years, Washington wrote in his diary,

"Dined with only Mrs. Washington, which I believe is the first instance of it since my retirement from public life."

This furlough, as the general used to speak of it, was not destined to continue overlong. The federation of the states proved too weak a government, and Washington must go to Philadelphia for months, to sit as president of the Constitutional Convention. Then after the people had ratified the Constitution, there came one day riding up the broad drive at Mount Vernon the aged secretary of Congress, with a letter notifying George Washington that he had been elected president of the United States.

"I little thought when the war was finished," wrote Martha Washington, "that any circumstances could possibly have happened which would call the General into public life again. I had anticipated that we should have been left to grow old in solitude and tranquillity together. That was the first and dearest wish of my heart . . . Yet I can not blame him for having acted according to his ideas of duty in obeying the voice of his country."

Alone to New York for the inauguration went George Washington, wearing a homespun suit woven at Mount Vernon. When his wife, likewise dressed in homespun, followed a few weeks later, her welcome all along the journey was second only to his. She entered many a town between two long columns of Revolutionary soldiers; and at New York City she was rowed across the bay by thirteen oarsmen dressed in white, while the guns fired thirteen rounds and crowds cheered her.

As the president's wife, Martha Washington was hostess for the nation, entertaining distinguished citizens and foreigners, cabinet officers and congressmen, presiding at the state dinners and giving public receptions every Friday, where

plum cake, tea and coffee were served. The
guests were always dismissed before nine, with
her grave, frank little formula, "For the general
always retires at nine, and I usually precede him."
The need over, she laid aside her homespun and
dressed in silk, satin, velvet and lace, as became
the wife of the president.

People criticized Mrs. Washington for the ceremony in force at her levees, saying they were too
much like those of royalty. Guests were shocked
because they had to stand, while the truth was,
the rooms would not have contained a third
enough chairs. Presided over by the Washingtons, the executive mansion combined with the
most ardent patriotism a dignity and elegant mod-
eration that would have honored any European
court. They saved the social life of a new country
from both the crudeness and bald simplicity of
extreme republicanism, and from the luxury and
excesses often marking sudden elevation to power
and place. And in all these social functions Mrs.
Washington never joined in any political discussion. Though the letters between her and her
husband were filled with talk of public affairs, she

was never once heard to utter any opinion on important questions of state; and in this, as in many details of her life, she is a worthy model for any American woman whose husband is in public service.

The year in New York was followed by similar years in Philadelphia, after the capital was moved there. The second term of the presidency over and a third term refused, the Washingtons gladly returned to Virginia; their joy being evidenced in this letter:

"I can not tell you how much I enjoy home, after having been deprived of one so long, for our dwelling in New York and Philadelphia was not home, only sojourning. The General and I feel like children just released from school or from a hard taskmaster, and we believe that nothing can tempt us to leave the sacred roof tree again, except on private business or pleasure. I am fairly settled down to the pleasant duties of an old-fashioned Virginia housekeeper, steady as a clock, busy as a bee, and cheerful as a cricket."

Happily they lived at Mount Vernon two years, until the general's death. During his brief illness Mrs. Washington never left his room.

" 'Tis well," were his last words.

"Is he dead?" she asked, so gentle had been the change. " 'Tis well. All is over now. I shall soon follow him. I have no more trials to pass through."

She moved up to a little attic room whose windows looked out toward his grave, and beyond to the waters of the Potomac which he had so loved. Surrounded by her grandchildren and great-grandchildren, cheerful in her sorrow and loneliness, she survived him two years, and when she died, was buried beside him in the simple brick tomb at Mount Vernon.

A woman not wise nor great perhaps in any worldly sense, Martha Washington had those qualities of heart that make a noble rounded character. A devoted and loyal wife, a tender mother, an earnest Christian, she was fitted to be the chosen companion of "the greatest of our soldiers and the purest of our patriots" Serene and kindly, in the familiar white cap and kerchief, she has become the nation's ideal of the president's wife, our country's first hostess.

CHAPTER VII

JEMIMA JOHNSON

1753-1814

OF Jemima Johnson, pioneer and volunteer, I can tell you very little. Just this one incident has come down to us, but you are surely right in thinking that the rest of her life was in harmony with this day's heroism.

It happened in Kentucky, when the Revolutionary fighting was almost ended, but before peace had come to the frontier. Raid after raid on isolated settlements was made by the Indians, stirred up continually by the British in Canada. People were murdered and tortured with shocking barbarity, for once started the red men could not be controlled. Chief among them were the Wyandottes, a tribe that stood first for military skill and ferocious valor, and with them was the notorious renegade, Simon Girty, whose name was a byword and a hissing along the frontier.

Bryan's Station was a Kentucky settlement of

forty cabins connected by strong palisades, set in a clearing with thick woods all around. One August day in 1782 messengers arrived, saying that the Indians were threatening to attack a neighboring fort and asking for aid. The men at Bryan's made ready to go and at dawn Captain Craig had finished his preparations when he discovered a group of savages in full view, just on the edge of the woods. There were only a few of them, and being out of rifle range they were exposing themselves carelessly and indifferently.

"They're trying to attract our attention," Craig immediately said to himself. "Do they think that because they're few we'll leave the fort and pursue them?"

Their actions made him suspicious, for he had been trained in Indian fighting in the school of Daniel Boone. He ordered the relief party to wait while he called the principal men of the station to a council. They agreed that it was only a feint on the part of the savages to invite an attack, and that the main fight would come from the other side. They would meet one trick with another and beat the Indians at their own game.

73

But the siege would be severe, perhaps long.
Nothing could be done until they had a supply of
water—and the spring was not inside the palisade, as was the frontier custom, but a short distance away, near the very spot where the red men
were hiding in the thick woods. The night before
only the ordinary amount of water had been
brought in. The buckets were empty, and it was
a hot August day. Life inside the stockade, even
though there were no battle, would be unendur-
able. Captain Craig thought a moment, then
called up the women and children, and told them
his plan.

"Will you, you women and you children who
are large enough, go down to the spring, with
every bucket you can carry, and bring back water?
Our lives depend upon it. We think the Indians
are hidden near the spring, waiting. Now if
you'll go, just as you do every morning, I
think they'll not molest you, for that would break
up their plan. As far as we can we'll cover you
with our rifles. You see, don't you, that this is
our only hope? If we men go to the spring, it
would be so unusual that it would rouse their sus-

Captain Craig called up the women and children and told them
his plan. "Our lives depend upon it."

picions at once; and if we were shot down, there would be no one to save the fort and you. Will you go?"

They were quick to appreciate the situation. Of course Captain Craig might be all wrong in his theory. The savages might capture the women and children, right under the eyes of the men in the fort. No one could tell what they might do. It was a terrible state of affairs. They knew what capture meant—death by torture. They had not lived on the frontier for nothing. A shudder of terror went through the group.

Water we must have.

The men can't go for it.

We women will.

Such were the steps Jemima Johnson's thoughts took, and instantly she volunteered. The Spartan daughter of a fearless pioneer, the sister of others, the wife of another, Jemima Suggett Johnson was also the mother of five little children, and her husband was away in Virginia. But she was the first to offer to go.

Quickly she gave her orders: Betsy, who was ten, was to go with her; Sally, to look after the two little boys as well as watch baby Richard, in his cradle. Now who would go with her for the water?

Armed with wooden dippers, the wives of the Craig brothers and their children volunteered. Others quickly offered. Captain Craig opened the gate and out they marched after Captain Johnson —twelve women and sixteen children—true helpmates of those sturdy frontiersmen. They were nearly overcome with terror, yet they laughed and chatted as they tramped down the hill some sixty yards to the spring. A few of the younger ones found it hard to hide their agitation, but Jemima Johnson's steadiness and cool composed manner reassured them and completely deceived the savages.

Within a stone's throw the Indians were concealed, and with eager covetous eyes watched the women filling their buckets. It took some time to dip up water for so many, but Captain Johnson had said each must wait until they were all ready to start back. Then deliberately they made their way up the hill to the fort, and not a shot was fired, for the Indians, in the hope of carrying out their original plan, did not betray their presence.

Some of the children, as they neared the gate, broke into a run and crowded into the door of the stockade, but only a little of the precious water was spilled. With sighs of relief the fifty men in the fort saw their wives and children safe again, and the supply of water stored away.

Then Captain Craig began to carry out his part of the scheme. Thirteen of his men were sent to the front of the fort, to engage the Indians there, with as much noise and confusion as possible. This, he guessed, was the signal agreed upon for the main body of savages to attack at the back of the stockade. So at the loopholes there he posted the rest of his men, with strict orders to make no move, to fire not a gun, till he gave them word. Hearing the noise at the front of the fort, the Indians near the spring dashed from cover and up to the back wall, which they supposed was undefended. They shouted their savage war cries, expecting an easy victory. Then suddenly the stockade bristled with rifles, and a steady fire was poured into the Indians massed for the attack. With cries of terror they fled to the woods; but all day long the firing continued. Deaths in the fort were very few, but any Indian who exposed himself was sure to be killed by the unerring shot of a frontiersman. Two savages climbed a tree, to fire from there, but were quickly dislodged. They shot burning arrows up into the air, to fall on the roofs of the buildings, but the plucky children put out the fires as fast as they were started. Betsy Johnson even tossed one arrow off baby Richard's cradle. The women who had brought the water that made this long defense possible, molded bullets and loaded rifles, repaired breaches in the palisade, and sometimes took their places at the loopholes.

At last the Indians decided their efforts could not succeed, so they killed the cattle, burned the fields of grain, and made the country look like a desert. Then they stole away in the night.

Thus Bryan's Station was saved, due in large measure to Jemima Johnson and her party of women who brought in the water. Years later the baby Richard commanded the Kentucky regiment whose brilliant charge decided the battle of the Thames. He, it was believed, killed the Indian chief Tecumseh. And this same son of Jemima Johnson became vice-president of the United States.

CHAPTER VIII

SACAJAWEA

1790-1884

DURING the last years of the eighteenth century, in an Indian village along the banks of the Snake River, just west of the Bitter Root Mountains, in what is now the state of Idaho, a little girl was born. She was named Sacajawea (Sah-cah"-jah-we'ah), which in English means "Bird-woman." Of her early life there is little to tell. She doubtless lived as did the rest of her tribe, grinding corn into meal, providing the food, always out-of-doors, alert and resourceful.

When she was about nine years old the Shoshones (or Snake Indians, as they were sometimes called) were attacked suddenly by their hereditary foe, the Minnetarees of Knife River They hastily retreated three miles up-stream and concealed themselves in the woods, but the enemy pursued. Being too few to contend successfully, the Shoshone men mounted their horses and fled, while the women and children scattered, but were soon captured. Sacajawea tried to escape by crossing the river at a shallow place, but half-way over was taken prisoner.

Eastward the captives were hurried, to a Minnetaree village near the present city of Bismarck, North Dakota, and here the girl Sacajawea was sold as a slave to Toussaint Chaboneau, a French half-breed, a wanderer and interpreter for the Northwest Fur Company. When she was about fourteen, an age considered womanhood among the Indians, Chaboneau married her.

In October of that year, 1804, there was much excitement in the village. Up the river from the south came a great boat, filled with white men, who, finding a good site for their camp on an island not far from the Minnetaree wigwams, landed, built a number of log huts and remained throughout the winter. From all the region roundabout the inquisitive Indians were continually visiting these white men whose errand was strange though peaceable. Not to make war, but to travel far to the west had they come. Among their supplies were many things about which the savages were curious. The squaws particularly were attracted by a mill that would grind their maize, enviously comparing its ease and speed with their slow methods. They longed for many articles in the white men's packs, and were glad to barter their corn for blue and white beads, for rings and for cloth. There was constant trading, and many, many were the questions asked about the great unknown country to the north and west.

A Canadian half-breed served the two white leaders of the party as interpreter. They also talked through Chaboneau, who knew both French and an Indian dialect, and who one day pointed out Sacajawea to them saying proudly, "She my slave, I buy her from de Rock Mountain, I make her my wife." When they heard who the Birdwoman was, they invited her and her husband to go with them on their long journey. He could interpret for some of the tribes, she for the Shoshones, for she had not forgotten the language of her childhood.

On the eleventh of February Sacajawea's son Baptiste was born, and a merry little papoose he proved to be. The travelers started west on

the seventh of April, Chaboneau accompanying
them, and Sacajawea carrying her baby, not quite
two months old; every step of that five-thousand-
mile journey she carried him, so that he was the
most traveled papoose in the land.

Taking the Bird-woman' with them was an extremely wise measure on the part of the leaders,
Lewis and Clark. Her presence was a sure guar-
antee that their intentions were peaceful, for no
Indian tribe ever took a woman in their war parties. For the whole group of men the presence of this gentle, virtuous, retiring little woman
and her baby must have had a softening, human-
izing effect, greater than they were aware. Near
the fire she would sit, making moccasins and
crooning a song in her soft Indian monotone,
while the baby toddled about, the two giving a
touch of domesticity to that Oregon winter.

There were many heroes of this journey to the
Far West, but only one heroine—this modest, un-
selfish, tireless squaw. With the strongest of the
men she canoed and trudged and climbed and
starved, always with the baby strapped on her
back. Long dreary months of toil she endured

like a Spartan. Instead of being a drag on their progress she was time and again the inspiration, the genius of the expedition. And in their journals both Lewis and Clark gave her frequent credit for her splendid services and frankly acknowledged in terms of respect and admiration their indebtedness to her.

One May afternoon when the travelers had been five or six weeks on their journey and were making good time with a sail hoisted on their boat, a sudden squall of wind struck them. The boat nearly went over, for Chaboneau, who was an interpreter and not a helmsman, lost his head, let go the tiller and called loudly to God for mercy. The water poured in and the boat was almost capsized before the men could cut the sail down. Out on the stream floated valuable papers and instruments, books, medicine, and a great quantity of merchandise. Always plucky in trouble, Sacajawea, who was in the rear, saved nearly all of these things, which were worth far more than their intrinsic value, since to replace them meant a journey of three thousand miles and a year's delay. No wonder that Clark added, when speak-

There was more than one hero of this journey to the Far West, but only one heroine—Sacajawea.

ing of the quick action of the Bird-woman, "to whom I ascribe equal fortitude and resolution with any person on board at the time of the accident."

Soon after this, from the tenth of June to the twenty-fourth, Sacajawea was very ill. One of the white captains bled her, a process that must have seemed strange to the Indian girl, but from their journals one can see that excellent care was taken of her. The party must continue on its way, so she was moved into the back part of the boat which was covered over and cool. All one night the Bird-woman complained, refusing the medicine offered her, while Chaboneau made constant petition to be allowed to return with his squaw.

The leaders were concerned for Sacajawea for they knew enough of medicine to see that her case was serious. And they were also concerned for the expedition's sake, for she was their sole dependence to negotiate with the Shoshone Indians on whom they relied for help. Lewis therefore determined to make camp till she was entirely restored. He persuaded her to take some laudanum and herbs and two days later wrote in his diary:

"Indian woman much better to-day. Continued same course of medicine. She is free from pain, clear of fever, her pulse regular, eats as heartily as I am willing to permit her of broiled buffalo well seasoned with pepper and salt and rich soup of the same meat."

The next day she improved rapidly, sat up for a time and even walked out. But alas! this brief period of convalescence Sacajawea evidently thought sufficient, and the following morning she

"walked out and gathered a considerable quantity of white apples of which she ate so heartily in their raw state, together with a considerable quantity of dried fish without my knowledge that she complained very much and her fever returned. I rebuked Chaboneau severely for suffering her to indulge herself with such food, and gave her diluted nitre and thirty drops of laudanum."

The next day, however, she appeared to be in a fair way for recovery, walking about and fishing, so the party again started westward.

Nine days later, while Clark, Chaboneau and Sacajawea were making a portage, they noticed a black cloud coming up rapidly in the west. Hunting about for shelter they found a ravine protected by shelving rocks. Clark had laid aside his gun and compass, the Bird-woman her baby's extra clothes and his cradle, when suddenly rain fell in such a torrent that it washed down rocks and earth from higher up the gorge. A landslide followed but just before the heaviest part of it struck them, the white captain seized his gun in one hand and with the other dragged Sacajawea, her baby in her arms, up the steep bank. Chaboneau caught at her and pulled her along, but was too frightened to be of much help.

Down the ravine in a rolling torrent came the rain, with irresistible force, driving rocks and earth and everything before it. The water rose waist high and before Clark could reach the higher ground had ruined his watch. The compass and the cradle and the baby's clothes were washed away. By the time they reached the top of the hill the water was fifteen feet deep in the ravine. Anxious lest little Baptiste take cold and fearful that Sacajawea should suffer a relapse, Clark hurried the group to camp with all possible speed and gave the Indian woman a little spirits to revive her.

Toward the end of July they came to a country

which Sacajawea knew. At first she was guided by instinct, like a homing bird. Then she began to recognize familiar landmarks, for this was where she had lived as a little girl. Both as guide and interpreter she was now the leading individual in the party, and of invaluable service. Often the white men could not see plainly the buffalo paths and Indian trails, but she divined them immediately. During her childhood she had traveled this road often, for it was the great resort of the Shoshones who came there to gather quamash and to trap the beaver.

Reaching the three forks of the Missouri River she advised that they follow the southern branch, as that was the route her tribe always took when crossing into the plains. One of their camps, the Bird-woman said, was on the very spot where she herself had been taken prisoner.

"She showed no distress at these recollections," comments the record, "nor any joy at the prospect of being restored to her country, for she seems to possess the folly or philosophy of not suffering her feelings to extend beyond the anxiety of having plenty to eat and a few trinkets to wear."

But that Sacajawea had no emotions was

clearly a mistaken inference, for the journal, a few days later, has an interesting story to tell. Hoping to find an Indian trail that would lead to a tribe which could supply them guides and horses, they landed, resolved to succeed if it took a month's time. It seemed a forlorn search, but at all costs these two necessities must be had.

With Chaboneau and his wife, Clark was walking along the shore, the Indians a hundred yards ahead, when Sacajawea began to dance and show every mark of the most extravagant joy, turning round to the white captain, pointing to several Indians approaching them, and sucking her fingers to show that they belonged to her tribe. Suddenly a woman made her way through the crowd, ran toward her and embraced her with the most tender affection. Companions in childhood, they had been taken prisoner at the same time and had shared captivity. Finally the one had escaped, while the other was left to be sold as a slave to the half-breed interpreter. A peculiarly touching meeting this was, for they had scarcely hoped ever to see each other again, and now they were renewing their friendship.

The two white captains meanwhile had a long conference with the Shoshone chief. After smoking together, gifts were exchanged. Then in order to converse more intelligently, Sacajawea was sent for. She sat down and began to translate, when, looking intently at the Indian chief, she recognized him as her brother. Jumping up she ran to him, embraced him, threw her blanket over him and wept. The chief himself was moved. Sacajawea tried to go on with her work of interpretation, but seemed overpowered by the situation and was frequently interrupted by tears.

Cameahwait, the Shoshone chief, agreed to aid the white men, giving them horses and guides, in which business Sacajawea was of the greatest help. She had a long talk with her brother, telling him of the great power of the American government, of the advantages he would receive by trading with the whites, and completely won the good will of her nation as she did that of other tribes they met. She persuaded her people to make the white men's journey through their country possible.

Now the chief wealth of the Shoshone Indians

was in their small wiry horses, fleet and sure-footed. Fine presents the white chiefs gave in exchange for pack-horses—an axe, a knife, a handkerchief and a little paint, all for one horse. As long as the supply of kettles held out, a kettle and a white pony were considered an even trade. Sometimes instead of the coveted kettle Claik would give a sword, a hundred bullets and powder, with some additional small articles. Once three horses were bargained for with one of the Indians, who left, the proud possessor of a chief's coat, handkerchiefs, a shirt, leggings and a few arrow points. One day after many wares were offered in exchange for otter skins, Sacajawea gave the precious beads which she wore around her waist.

The Bird-woman was invaluable also as an interpreter. The captains would speak in English, which was put into French by one of the men, Chaboneau then repeated it in the Minnetaree dialect to his wife, who translated it into the Shoshone tongue which was understood by an Indian boy in the party, and he in turn told it to the tribe with whom Lewis and Clark wished to talk. Do you wonder that when possible they all used sign language, and relied still more on the language of gifts?

The Americans were surprised that Sacajawea showed no desire to remain with her own people, but her loyalty and devotion to the explorers were unfailing. Once she learned of threatened treachery on the part of her tribe, that they planned to break camp and go down the Missouri River to the buffalo country on the east, taking with them the horses which had been promised to the white men. This would leave the newcomers stranded in the mountains, the lack of horses preventing their going westward. Immediately she told Lewis and Clark, who called the chiefs together, and after some discussion the plan was changed. By the end of August, with a replenished larder and fresh horses, the explorers were ready to start once more on their journey westward.

The road, Sacajawea told the white captains, was over steep and rocky mountains, in whose fastnesses they would come to the narrow divide marking the source of the Missouri River. An hour later they would find a stream running west, that would grow into a large river and flow on till it came to the great waters far away. But there was no food along its course, no paths along its rocky banks, no canoes could swim on its rough current. If they went on they must follow rude Indian trails where there was no game. For ten days they must cross a sandy desert. In many places travel would be slow.

Slow progress indeed it was, on this toilsome, dangerous journey. Some days five miles was the best they could make; other days they went forward scarcely at all. Food became scarce, and among the men, as winter weather came on, there was much sickness. Once they had a six-day storm that drenched everything they had on. And by this time their supply of dried meat and fish was exhausted.

They followed obscure windings of Indian trails, known only to the savages. Sometimes they made their way through wild cañons strewn with stones; sometimes they climbed painfully up a rough slippery height, or skirted the edge of a precipice. Almost a month was spent in getting

93

through the mountains. Cold, half-starved, fatigued, ragged, footsore, they came out on the other side, more like fugitives than conquerors.

What would they have done without Sacajawea? Dauntless and determined, always cheerful and resourceful, she had in her care the lives and fortunes of the whole party. It was she who gathered plants unknown to the white captains and cooked them into a mush. It was she who varied their monotonous diet by roasting, boiling and drying fennel roots, and stewing wild onions with their meat. It was she who found berries and edible seeds when starvation seemed the only outcome. She searched in the prairie dogs' holes with a sharp stick and discovered wild artichokes, as valuable as potatoes, with a delicious flavor. She taught the white men how to break shank bones of elk, boil them and extract the grease to make "trapper's butter." When Clark was ill she made bread for him with some flour she had saved for her baby—the only mouthful he tasted for days.

Late in November they reached the coast and spent the winter, a forlorn group, at Fort Clatsop.

There was much sickness and the strength of the men began to fail. There was nothing but dried fish for food, and it rained and rained till their clothes and bedding rotted away.

They had a strange celebration on Christmas day, when the men sang songs in the morning, and the Bird-woman brought a gift to Clark—two dozen white weasels' tails!

In January during a brief interval of sunny weather, they planned to go to the beach to get oil and blubber from a whale that was reported stranded there. Sacajawea had heard of the Pacific in the legends of her tribe, she had heard of whales too, and begged to be allowed to go. Had she traveled all that long way only to fail to see the great waters and the great fish? So Clark agreed that she should accompany them. When they arrived the Indians had already disposed of the whale, the skeleton, a hundred and five feet long, being all that was left.

Because of sickness and scant stores of food, bitterly disappointed when no trading ships appeared with fresh supplies, they began the return trip early in March instead of in April. Progress was so rapid that the journey which westward had lasted for full eight months, was made in five, and six weeks of this time was taken up by a detour. The party divided and Clark, with Chaboneau and Sacajawea as guides, went to explore the Yellowstone.

In August they were once more at the Minnetaree village where the Bird-woman had first seen the white captains and their mill for grinding corn. Here the leaders said good-by to their Indian friend and guide. Clark offered to take the family to the states, give them land, horses, cows and hogs to start farming, or a boatload of merchandise as a stock for trading. But Chaboneau preferred to remain among the Indians, saying he had no acquaintance in the East and no chance of making a livelihood. Clark then offered to take the baby, "my little dancing boy Baptiest," now eighteen months old, and bring him up as his own child, but Sacajawea refused.

Chaboneau's wages, together with the payment for a horse, were five hundred dollars and thirty-three cents. The records say not a word of any sum for Sacajawea whose faithfulness and intelligence had made success possible. She who could divine routes, who had courage when the men quailed, who could spread as good a table with bones as others with meat, was unthought of when bounties in land and money were granted.

Writing back to Chaboneau a few days later, Clark did indeed give her full credit when he said:

"Your woman who accompanied you that long and dangerous and fatiguing route to the Pacific Ocean and back deserved a greater reward for her attention and services on that route than we had in our power to give her at the Mandans."

Chaboneau's money probably served to establish his family very comfortably in the village in Dakota. You can imagine what stories they told of their adventures during the long winter evenings—of the wild animals they met, of their escape from the cloudburst at the Great Falls, of the mysterious, explosive sounds heard in the mountains, of the portages they made, of shooting the rapids in the Columbia, of their struggle among the snows of the Bitter Root range, and of the great salt ocean at the sunset—for they had taken part in the most remarkable exploration of modern times.

For many years there is no record of Sacajawea. Clark, as superintendent of Indian affairs, in 1837 appointed Chaboneau interpreter, with a salary of three hundred dollars. And there is one official item, an expense account for a boy (possibly Baptiste) in school at Saint Louis, which was paid to Chaboneau, in 1820. The little papoose who traveled all that long journey grew up to be a guide, with his mother's native instinct and cleverness. He served with Bridger in southwest Wyoming; he is mentioned with Fremont in 1842 and from sometime in the sixties he lived on an Indian reservation in Fremont County, Wyoming.

Sacajawea was there with him after 1871. An old, old woman, she is described by one of the missionaries, Doctor Irwin, short of stature, spare of figure, quick in her movements, remarkably straight and wonderfully active and intelligent considering her great age. She often told of her journey to the place of "much water

for the great Washington," as the government
was always referred to, and talked of the "big
waters beyond the shining mountains, toward the
setting sun." And on that reservation she died
and was buried.

The journey of the two white captains pushed
the frontier from the Mississippi to the coast. It
burst through the Rocky Mountain barrier and
opened the gates to the Pacific slope. It gave
the nation a rich territory from which ten states
were formed. But the services of Sacajawea
had for many years no lasting commemoration.
Shortly after the adventure in the boat the leaders
did indeed name a river for the Bird-woman, one
of the branches of the Musselshell in central Montana, but the very first settlers changed it from
Sacajawea to Crooked Creek and so it is called
to-day. In very recent times the Geological Sur-
vey named for her the great peak in the Bridger
range overlooking the spot where she was captured, and where she pointed out the pass over the
mountains—a route chosen years later by the en-
gineers of the Northern Pacific Railroad. This
place was also marked with a boulder and

tablet by the Montana chapter of the Daughters of the Revolution.

That is all that remains of Sacajawea—a peak bearing her name, and her story. A century after her long journey the women of Oregon erected, in the center of the great exposition court at Portland, a bronze statue of the noble Indian girl whose faithful service as a guide made possible the success of the Lewis and Clark Expedition.

CHAPTER IX

DOLLY MADISON

1772-1836

DOLLY PAYNE was a Virginian, though she was born while her parents were on a visit in North Carolina. She lived on a great plantation where she had wide fields to play in, and a devoted black mammy to look after her. Both her mother and grandmother were noted belles and Dolly, who was named for her second cousin, Mrs. Patrick Henry, evidently inherited their beauty, for as a very little girl, going to school, she wore a wide-brimmed sunbonnet and long mitts, to shield her face and arms from the sun.

Dolly remembered how her father, in spite of the fact that they were Quakers, had buckled on his sword and ridden away to be a captain in the Revolutionary army, and how when the war was over, he came home again to join in the neighborhood's thanksgiving for America.

Soon after the war, when Dolly was fourteen years old, he freed his slaves, sold the
plantation, and moved north to the city of brotherly love that he might be among Quakers. It
was then the largest town in the nation, with a
reputation for being very rich and gay. But the
Paynes maintained a strict Quaker standard of
simplicity.

Dorothy was a pretty girl, demure in her gray
dress, but with bright Irish-blue eyes, long lashes,
curling black hair and soft warm-hued skin. She
had a particularly gay and joyous disposition, but
was forbidden such pleasures as dancing and
music. She went to the Friends' meeting-house
where the men and boys in their black coats and
broad-brimmed hats sat on one side of the room,
the women and girls in their mouse-colored bon-
nets and drab gowns on the other.

Dolly's father had done very well on the southern plantation, but when he went into business in
Philadelphia he found many troubles. Living
cost much more than in Virginia, a good deal of
his property had been lost through the war and
he failed, then ill health added its burden. A

rich young Quaker lawyer named John Todd
helped and advised him. He had fallen in love
with Dolly, and though she meant never to marry,
she consented, to please her father who had only a
few months more to live.

On two successive Sundays she went through
the embarrassing Quaker ceremony of rising in
meeting and saying she proposed taking John
Todd in marriage; and standing up before the
congregation, they were married in the somber
bare-walled meeting-house. Mistress Todd lived
for three years the life of a Quaker lady, and a
devoted wife she was to her young husband. She
always wore a cap of tulle, a gray gown, with a
lace kerchief over her shoulders and a large brooch
fastening it—no other ornaments. Except for
her beauty she was like a hundred other young
Quaker women in the city of brotherly love.

In August of 1793 an epidemic of yellow fever
broke out in Philadelphia. Todd sent his wife
and their two little children to a summer resort
on the river, where many of their friends took
refuge. He stayed in the city to care for his
father and mother but they died of the plague.

Already ill himself he joined his family, only to give them the dread disease, he and the baby dying shortly after his arrival. Dolly too was stricken with the fever, but recovered.

At first she was bowed down by her great loss. But Philadelphia was gay and gradually Mistress Todd began going about again, far more freely than in the days of her sober girlhood. She found herself really enjoying society and all the pleasures of the city. From a shy girl she developed into a most attractive woman. With her youth and her riches, it is no wonder that she became the object of much attention. Gentlemen would station themselves to see her pass, and her friends would say, "Really, Dolly, thou must hide thy face. There are so many staring at thee!"

Among her many admirers was Aaron Burr, then a United States senator. For Philadelphia, you remember, was the capital of the newly organized government, and the leading men of the time lived in the city. One day he asked her if he might bring a friend to call, for the "great little Madison," as his colleagues called him, had requested the honor of being presented. So the handsome Colonel Burr introduced Mr. James Madison, a little man dressed all in black, except for his ruffled shirt and silver buckles. Dolly wore a mulberry satin gown with silk tulle about her neck and a dainty lace cap on her head, her curly hair showing underneath. The scholarly Madison, who was twenty years older than she, was captivated by the pretty widow, sparkling with fun and wit, and soon offered himself as a husband, and was accepted.

The President and Mrs. Washington were much pleased when they heard of the engagement. Sending for Dolly Mrs. Washington asked her if the news was true.

"No, I think not," said Mistress Todd.

"Be not ashamed to confess it, if it is so. He will make thee a good husband and all the better for being so much older. We both approve of it. The esteem and friendship existing between Mr. Madison and my husband is very great, and we would wish you two to be happy."

Happy they were, during the week's journey when they drove down to Virginia, to be married at the home of Dolly's sister; and during the merrymaking following the wedding which lavish southern hospitality, with a ball and feast after the ceremony, made quite different from her first marriage. The quiet reserved Madison let the girls cut off bits of his Mechlin lace ruffles as keepsakes. And happy they were together for more than forty years.

They lived only a short time at Montpelier, Madison's home in the Blue Ridge country, for public affairs soon took them back to Philadelphia and then to Washington. At her husband's request Dolly laid aside her Quaker dress, entered society and entertained frequently. Her sweet manners, her tact and kindness of heart, made her friends everywhere. At that time party spirit ran high and political differences caused great bitterness, but all animosities seemed forgotten in Mrs. Madison's presence. She slighted no one, hurt no one's feelings, and often made foes into friends. Perhaps her influence had almost as much to do with Madison's prominence in national affairs as did his own unquestioned ability; for her sound common sense and exceptionally good judgment often helped him in deciding public questions.

When Jefferson was elected president he made Madison his secretary of state. And since Jefferson was a widower and needed a lady to preside at the White House, he often called upon Mrs. Madison for this service. Then Madison succeeded Jefferson and Dolly became in name what she had been in effect, the first lady of the land. Thus for sixteen years she was hostess for the nation, and a famous hostess she was indeed.

"Every one loves Mrs. Madison," said Henry Clay, voicing the common sentiment.

"And Mrs. Madison loves everybody," was her quick response.

The president used to say that when he was tired out from matters of state a visit to her sitting-room, where he was sure of a bright story and a hearty laugh, was as refreshing as a long walk in the open air.

But even with such a mistress of the White House the affairs of the nation did not remain tranquil. Trouble with England, which had long been brewing, came to a crisis and war was declared in 1812. As most of the fighting was at sea, life at Washington went on undisturbed until August of 1814, when the British landed five thousand men near the capital and marched to attack it. The town was in a panic when the messenger rode in at full speed, announcing fifty ships anchoring in the Potomac.

"Have you the courage to stay here till I come back, to-morrow or next day?" asked the president.

And Dolly Madison replied, "I am not afraid of anything, if only you are not harmed and our army triumphs."

"Good-by then, and if anything happens, look out for the state papers," said Madison, and rode away to the point where the citizen-soldiers were gathering.

Many Washington people began carrying their property off to the country, but the brave woman at the White House did not run away. At last there came a penciled note from the president:

"Enemy stronger than we heard at first. They may reach the city and destroy it. Be ready to leave at a moment's warning."

Most of Mrs. Madison's friends were already gone, even the soldiers who had been left to guard the executive mansion. Not a wagon could be secured. "Bring me as many trunks as my carriage will hold," ordered Dolly Madison and set to work packing them with the nation's most valuable papers. Night came but the lady of the White House worked on. At dawn she began searching through her spyglass, hoping to catch a glimpse of her husband. All she could see was here and there a group of soldiers wandering about, men sleeping in the fields, frightened women and children hurrying to the bridge over the Potomac. She could hear the roar of cannon, the battle was going on only six miles away; still the president did not come.

One of the servants, French John, offered to spike the cannon at the gate and lay a train of powder that would blow up the British if they entered the house. But to this Mrs. Madison objected, though she could not make John understand why in war every advantage might not be taken.

About three o'clock in the afternoon two men

covered with dust galloped up and cried, "Fly, fly! The house will be burned over your head!"

Some good friends had succeeded in getting a wagon and Mrs. Madison filled it with the White House silver.

"To the bank of Maryland," she ordered, and added to herself, "or the hands of the British— which will it be?"

Two friends came in to urge haste, reminding her that the English admiral, Cockburn, had taken an oath that he would sit in her drawing-room and that other officers had boasted they would take the president and his wife both prisoner and carry them to London to make a show of them. They were just ready to lift her into the carriage when Dolly stopped.

"Not yet—the portrait of Washington—it shall never fall into the hands of the enemy. That must be taken away before I leave the house."

The famous painting by Gilbert Stuart was in a heavy frame, screwed to the wall in the state dining-room, but in that frantic hurry there were no tools at hand to remove it.

"Get an axe and break the frame," commanded

Dolly Madison. She watched the canvas taken from the stretcher, saw it rolled up carefully, and sent to a place of safety. Later it was returned to her, and to-day hangs over the mantel in the red room of the White House.

One more delay—the Declaration of Independence was kept in a glass case, separate from the other state papers. Notwithstanding all the protests of her friends, Dolly Madison ran back into the house, broke the glass, secured the Declaration with the autographs of the signers, got into her carriage and drove rapidly away to a house beyond Georgetown.

None too soon did she leave. The sound of approaching troops was heard. The British were upon the city. They broke into the executive mansion, ransacked it, had dinner there in the state dining-room, stole what they could carry, and then set fire to the building.

Instead of sleeping that night, Dolly Madison, with thousands of others, watched the fire destroying the capital, while the wind from an approaching storm fanned the flames. Before daybreak she set out for a little tavern, sixteen miles away, where her husband had arranged to meet her. The roads were filled with frightened people, while fleeing soldiers spread the wildest rumors of the enemy's advance.

Arrived at the inn finally in the height of the storm, the woman in charge refused to take her in, saying, "My man had to go to fight; your husband brought on this war and his wife shall have no shelter in my house!"

The tavern was thronged with women and children, refugees from the city, who finally prevailed on the woman to let Mrs. Madison enter. The president arrived later, but before he had rested an hour a messenger came crying, "The British know you are here—fly!"

Dolly Madison begged him to go to a little hut in the woods where he would be safe, and promised that she would leave in disguise and find a refuge farther away. In the gray of the morning she started, but soon came the good news that the English, hearing reinforcements were coming, had gone back to their ships. At once she turned and drove toward the city. The bridge over the Potomac was afire.

"Will you row me across?" she asked an American officer.

"No, we don't let strange women into the city." In vain she pleaded. He was firm. "We have spies enough here. How do I know but the British have sent you to burn what they have left? You will not cross the river, that is sure."

"But I am Mrs. Madison, the wife of your president," she answered, throwing off her disguise. Then he rowed her across the Potomac. Through clouds of smoke, past heaps of still smoldering ruins, she made her way to the home of her sister, and waited there for Mr. Madison to return.

While the White House was being rebuilt the Madisons lived in Pennsylvania Avenue, and a brilliant social life centered about them. They revived the levees of Washington and Adams, gave handsome state dinners and introduced music at their receptions.

When Madison's second term was ended they went to live at Montpelier, their beautiful Virginia home, where they entertained with true southern hospitality the many friends and tourists who visited them. Mr. Madison, for many years an invalid, busied himself with books and writing.

Soon after his death in 1836 Dolly returned to Washington, to be near her old friends. Her home again became a social center, for her tact and beauty and grace made her always a favorite and a leader. She entertained many distinguished guests, "looking every inch a queen," the British ambassador declared. Sometimes there were as many visitors at her receptions as at those at the White House. All the homage of former times was hers, and much consideration was shown her by public officials, Congress voting her a seat on the floor of the House.

Brought up in strict Quaker ways, she adorned every station in life in which she was placed. And in a crisis when the White House was in danger, Dolly Madison was courageous enough to delay her departure till she had saved the Stuart Washington and the Declaration of Independence.

CHAPTER X

LUCRETIA MOTT

1793-1880

LUCRETIA COFFIN was a Quaker, born on the quaint little island of Nantucket. Her father "followed the sea," captain of a whaler, and was often gone for long periods of time. So it was the mother who was responsible for the early training of the six children. Thrift and efficient housekeeping Lucretia learned, along with the Quaker doctrine of non-resistance, and a thorough knowledge of the Bible.

When she was twelve, Captain Coffin forsook the sea and moved his family to Boston. Public schools there gave Lucretia a feeling of sympathy for the patient struggling poor which was always a prominent trait in her character.

Later she was sent to a Friends' boarding-school at Nine Partners, New York, and stayed for two years, with no holidays and no vacation. A strict school it was, for though both boys and

115

girls were the pupils, they were not allowed to speak to each other unless they were near relatives in which case they might talk on certain days over the fence that separated their playgrounds. Punishment Lucretia Coffin could bear herself far more easily than she could see some one else endure it; when for some trifling misdemeanor, a little boy, a cousin of James Mott, one of the teachers, was locked up in a dark closet and given only bread and water, Lucretia managed to slip into the forbidden side of the house and supply him with more substantial food.

One of the instructors left the school, and fifteen-year-old Lucretia became an assistant teacher, working with her classes in the daytime, and with her books by the light of a solitary candle far into the night. A year later she was made a regular teacher, with a salary of a hundred dollars, her living and tuition for one of her little sisters.

The two young pedagogues, James Mott and Lucretia Coffin, found that they had many ideas in common—ability, and a desire for knowledge and a wider culture—so they formed a French class and had lessons for six weeks. Such good friends they became that when she was eighteen and he a few years older, they became engaged and were married and settled in Philadelphia. He was quiet, reserved, serious; she bright, active, very pretty. And after they had worked together for a great cause, they loved each other more deeply than ever.

As a very young girl Lucretia Mott had been interested in slavery. Her sympathy had first been enlisted from reading in her schoolbooks Clarkson's vivid picture of the slave ships. Many years later she repeated word for word a description of the horrors of the "middle passage," which she had memorized from a reader. In 1818 on a journey to Virginia, she had a first affecting glimpse of the slaves themselves.

This trip to the South was for the purpose of holding religious meetings, for early that year Lucretia Mott discovered her great gift—public speaking. Among the Friends it was no uncommon thing for women to take part in meeting, and Mrs. Mott soon became one of their favorite preachers. She had a real power over her au-

diences—her slight figure, her delicate, charming
face in the Quaker bonnet, at once strong and
tender, her sweetness of voice added to the con-
vincing earnestness of her manner.

People of all denominations went miles to hear
her. Soon she began traveling around the
country, speaking in Quaker meeting-houses, telling her listeners of the peace-loving principles of
the Friends, pointing out the evils of injustice in
any form, and always, in season and out of season, emphasizing the sin of slavery. Long
before Lundy and Garrison began their newspapers, long before Garrison and Wendell
Phillips were thundering against slavery and urg-
ing immediate emancipation, this small sweet-
faced Friend, mild and gentle in nature, was
blazing the way for the anti-slavery movement, a
pioneer among the advocates for freedom.

Through New York State, into New England
and across to Nantucket, as far south as Virginia,
west to Ohio and Indiana, she traveled by stage-
coach or boat or carriage. Speaking at seventy-
one meetings in a ten weeks' trip seems to have
been no unusual record for her. She always

wore a simple, dove-colored dress, with a crossed muslin kerchief at the neck, and a prim little cap. But the secret of her magnetic personality was that she spoke because she was conscious of a power impelling her to do so. Words came to her, as tears come, without will of her own, because her heart was full and she couldn't help it. Though the leading abolitionists were often described as raving fanatics, Lucretia Mott was noted for her unfailing composure, her calm tone of profound faith, her lack of vehement accents and violent gestures.

"Notice was given here for a religious meeting," said the distressed elders in one western town that bordered on a slave state. "We do hope, Mrs. Mott, you will not name slavery, or allude to it this afternoon."

"Why," was her answer, "that is eminently a religious subject. I should consider myself disobedient to the voice of God in my soul if I did not speak against it."

Her audience there was so large that many had to stand. Ordinarily they would have become restless. For an hour and a half she held them,

closely attentive, and though she said some
things far from palatable to that prejudiced, excited, border section, her sincerity commanded
their respect and they crowded the hall again that
evening to hear her speak.

Gradually the opposition to slavery, which she
had been fostering, won adherents to its cause.
The Garrison campaign began. Friends of freedom came out openly and spoke their views. In
1833 a national anti-slavery society was formed
in Philadelphia. Of the sixty or seventy delegates, four were women, Lucretia Mott among
them. They were present by invitation, as listeners only. But during the discussion of the
proposed constitution, when one of the women
briefly, modestly, suggested transposing certain
sentences, to put first the reference to the Declaration of Independence, the men were so impressed
that they made the change immediately. But more
than this Mrs. Mott, a listener, accomplished.
Her encouragement strengthened and confirmed
their purpose at a critical moment when some
overcautious souls urged a policy of delay.

The following year the Female Anti-slavery

Society was formed, the majority of its members Friends, and Lucretia Mott served as president during most of its existence. For women to have an association of their own was almost unheard of, in the eighteen thirties. They had no idea of the meaning of preambles, resolutions and voting; and later they confessed with amusement that they had to invite a colored man to preside at their first meeting, to get them started.

In 1840 came a world's anti-slavery convention in London, and Lucretia Mott was one of the delegates from the United States. Full of enthusiasm the first group arrived, only to find that women were not to be recognized. The doors were shut against them, because of the old, old prejudice—women should stay at home and be entertaining, public affairs would rob them of their sweetest charm.

Wendell Phillips protested and moved that the ladies be admitted. The excited discussion lasted for several hours, but when the vote was taken the majority against the resolution was overwhelming. So in the gallery sat Lucretia Mott, with Harriet Martineau, Mrs. Wendell

Phillips, and other women delegates, and their recruit, Elizabeth Cady Stanton.

Arriving some days later, Garrison felt so outraged at this treatment of his co-workers that he refused to take his seat in the convention. With two other masculine members from the American Society he sat up-stairs with the ladies. The British were scandalized—what sort of world's convention was this, with the founder of the greatest anti-slavery movement of the century debarred from taking his seat on the floor? They sent him a special invitation, but Garrison was firm. He remembered that Lucretia Mott had been the first to shake his hand when he came out of prison!

But before the meetings were over a tea was given with more than four hundred guests; and there, much to the men's consternation, Lucretia Mott spoke. With a dignity that carried great force, with real eloquence, she chose this way of addressing the convention. The delegates found themselves listening with pleasure and admiration, and broke into applause.

While they were in London, Lucretia Mott had

a call from Clarkson, the English abolitionist, then an old, old man of eighty-one, almost blind, and they had a long talk together.

It is difficult for people of to-day to appreciate what peril and reproach it meant to take a stand against slavery. Individuals who dared to do so had to face private detraction and public abuse, sometimes actual physical violence. On the side of slavery was ranged all the power of trade and politics, of church and state, of respectability and riot. This opposition became more and more bitter, more and more popular, more and more widely spread. In equal or greater ratio the earnestness and zeal of the anti-slavery group increased. They were held up to odium and ridicule, for the spirit of persecution was abroad. Lucretia Mott's old friends scorned her and laughed at her. They passed her on the street without speaking.

"But," said she, "misrepresentation and ridicule and abuse heaped on these reforms do not in the least deter me from my duty."

Mobs of men and women would assemble outside the halls where anti-slavery meetings were being held. They stoned the windows, they broke in, leaped on the platform, and shouted so loudly that the speaker's voice was lost in the noise. Pennsylvania Hall, dedicated to "liberty and the rights of man," was surrounded by a crowd while Lucretia Mott was addressing an audience of Philadelphia women, and brickbats were hurled through the windows. The next day, shortly after the meeting had adjourned, the mob set the hall on fire, then marched through the streets, threatening an attack on the Motts' house. The children were sent away to a place of safety, and the little Quaker lady, with her husband and a few friends, sat quietly waiting for the crowd to come. But their fury was turned against another part of the city and the Motts were safe for that night.

Shortly afterward they were sitting in the parlor one evening when they heard confused noises and cries that came nearer and nearer—an angry rumble hard to describe, but all too familiar to the experienced ears of negroes and abolitionists. In the crowd was a young man who knew the Quaker family. "On to the Motts'!" he cried, and purposely ran up the wrong street, making several quick turnings. The rioters followed him blindly until he slipped away from them, and a second time the Motts were saved from violence.

In New York City an anti-slavery meeting was broken up by the crowd and Garrison and other speakers roughly handled. Lucretia Mott, whose fears and thoughts were never for herself, always unshrinking and self-possessed in the stormiest scenes, noticed that some of the women looked timid.

"Won't thee look after the others?" she asked the gentleman who accompanied her.

"Then who will take care of you?"

"This man will see me through," she said, putting her hand on the arm of a big ruffian in a red shirt. Roused by this unexpected appeal to his chivalry he made way for her through the crowd and escorted her safely to the house where she was staying.

The next day in a restaurant near the hall, she recognized him and sitting down at his table began talking with him. When he left he asked:

"Who is that lady?"

"Lucretia Mott."

Dumfounded for a moment he shook his head and then said, "Well, she's a good sensible woman!"

In her own home Lucretia Mott sheltered fugitive slaves, till it became widely known as a place of refuge. Many a poor negro she helped on his way to Canada, by the Underground Railroad. In the entrance hall of the Mott house there stood two roomy armchairs which the family called "the beggars' chairs," for there applicants, rich and poor, known and unknown, black and white, waited to see Mrs. Mott.

Almost incredible was the opposition she met. Even the gentle Quakers reproached her for "lugging in" slavery at their meetings. Many of them wished she would resign. A minority wanted to disown her. They refused the use of their meeting-houses for abolition lectures. When she was speaking away from Philadelphia they allowed her to stay at country taverns, instead of inviting her to their homes—a great breach of hospitality. They discussed taking away her "approved minister's minute," which introduced

"Who will take care of you?"
"This man'll see me through," answered Lucretia Mott, putting
her hand on the arm of a big ruffian in a red shirt.

her to Quaker communities. But in justice to herself, and because she loved the society and its traditions and desired to remain a Friend, she was so careful that they could bring no case against her.

Never did she compromise her principles. Never did she ask for police protection, though the mob clamored and howled around the building. And never did she meet bodily harm. She lived the Quaker doctrine of non-resistance, and did not believe in repelling violence with violence. Holding that slavery was wrong, the Motts decided to use nothing made with slave labor. That meant giving up sugar and candy and cotton cloth. Most of all, it meant giving up the cotton goods commission business in which for the first time James Mott was finding it possible to make a comfortable living. Yet unflinchingly they sacrificed material prosperity for the spiritual gain. Mrs. Mott opened a school and they managed to get along until a new business could be established.

After the Civil War colored people were not allowed to ride in the Philadelphia street-cars except in certain ones reserved for them. One rainy day Lucretia Mott saw a negress, evidently in poor health, standing on the platform in a cold drizzle. She asked the conductor to let her enter the car, but he refused. Immediately Mrs. Mott went outside and stood by the woman. The famous Mrs. Mott, seventy years old, riding in the rain on the platform of his car? That would never do! The conductor begged her to come in.

"Not without this woman—I can not!" was the reply.

"Oh, well, bring her in then," he said. And soon the company changed the rule discriminating against colored passengers.

After the fugitive slave law was passed in 1850 many exciting cases came up in Philadelphia. Perhaps the most famous was the trial of a negro named Daniel Webster Dangerfield, who was arrested, charged with being a fugitive slave. The alleged master engaged a famous lawyer who was later attorney-general of the United States. The trial lasted all one day, into the night and the next day; all that time Lucretia Mott with her knitting sat in the crowded room beside the poor ragged prisoner, like a guardian spirit. The opposing counsel asked that her chair be moved, fearing that her face would influence the jury!

In the court the negro won; but outside a rabble surged up and down, threatening to give him over to his Maryland master, while inside a group of young Quakers was equally determined that he should keep his hard-won freedom. Another colored man, resembling him, was driven away from the court-house in the carriage, while Dangerfield walked a few squares with some of his friends, then was sent eight miles to an unsuspected station of the Underground Railroad, and in a few days was safe in Canada.

"I have heard a great deal of Mrs. Mott," said the opposing lawyer at the conclusion of the trial, "but never saw her before to-day. She is an angel!"

Soon after he joined the party of freedom. Asked how he dared to make the change, with so many interests arrayed on the other side, his answer was, "Do you think there is anything I dare not do, after sitting in that court room facing Lucretia Mott?"

With all her public work this gentle Friend was

first of all a womanly woman, a fine housekeeper, a splendid mother, a devoted wife. Her letters speak constantly of the varied activities of her hands—of doing the family ironing, making mince meat for forty pies, sewing and putting down carpets, knitting, and making carpet-rags and the children's clothes. She was herself the best answer to the argument that public affairs must necessarily take a woman's attention from her household.

For years the abolitionists felt their cause hopeless. The very utmost they could do would be a lifelong protest against slavery. But Lucretia Mott lived to see freedom for the negroes an accomplished fact. Nor did she confine her work to this one cause. She was as firm an advocate of woman's equality with man, an able speaker for woman's rights in that early day when the subject met only ridicule and abuse. She used her eloquence for temperance, for the advancement of the freedmen, for peace through arbitration.

Instead of averted faces and open condemnation, in her last years she met everywhere with tenderness and veneration. And her face was like that of a transfigured saint, for she was without jealousy or bitterness, free from malice, incapable of hate. She was a preacher, a reformer, a woman commanding our admiration.

Exactly how much she did for abolition in that half-century of agitation and reform can not be measured accurately. She planted the seed and encouraged others. As famous and as much abused as Garrison, as popular a speaker as Phillips, she antedated them both. She was a veritable pioneer in the great movement that culminated in Lincoln's Emancipation Proclamation.

CHAPTER XI

1811-1896

THE Beechers came to America in 1638 and were leaders in the New Haven colony. Almost two centuries later the most celebrated member of this family was born in the old parsonage in the beautiful Connecticut hilltown of Litchfield. The father of this little girl, Lyman Beecher, was preaching earnest sermons, on the munificent salary of five hundred a year. To add to their income the mother, a beautiful and gifted woman, opened a school, though she had eight children of her own to care for. All of them grew up to be distinguished, especially the two youngest, Harriet and Henry Ward, who were inseparable companions.

Harriet had a remarkable memory and read all the books she could find. But most of her father's library was sermons and church pamphlets, appeals and replies and theological discussions; so you can imagine her delight when at the bottom of a garret barrel of musty sermons and essays she discovered *The Arabian Nights,* and delicious fragments of *The Tempest* and *Don Quixote.* Her father had said his children were not to read novels, but made an exception of *Ivanhoe.* The delighted Harriet and her brother George read it through seven times in six months, until indeed they could recite many scenes by heart.

The Beecher children were wide-awake, bright, happy youngsters, a big family of them, partly educated by running wild on the long breezy hills. Until she was eleven Harriet went to a "dame school" and to the Litchfield Academy, showing her future bent by thoroughly enjoying, instead of dreading, the task of composition writing. Sir Walter Scott helped form her style. She read and re-read her few books until words and sentences were fixed in her mind.

At one of the school exhibitions when compositions were read, Doctor Beecher, listening idly, suddenly brightened and looked up.

"Who wrote that?" he asked.

"Your daughter, sir," replied the teacher.

"That," said Harriet years later, when she knew something of fame, "was the proudest moment of my life."

The older sister Catherine had opened a school for girls at Hartford, and twelve-year-old Harriet went there, first as a pupil, then as teacher. Indeed she was for a time both, and crowded days she had. In this double race for development her brain wearied out her body. The memory of those overworked days lingered with her all her life. Healthy and hearty as a little child, she was allowed to think and feel and study too much. Consequently as a woman she was far from vigorous, finding her lack of strength a continual drawback to her work.

Her father had been preaching for six years in Boston and was now offered the presidency of Lane Seminary, to be opened in Cincinnati. Catherine was to start a school for girls, with Harriet as her assistant. The whole family made the toilsome adventurous journey across the mountains by stage-coach, to what was then considered the Far West.

In addition to her work in the school Harriet wrote short essays and sketches for publication, giving them away at first. But when the *Western Magazine* offered a prize of fifty dollars for a story and she won it, she began to think of writing as a possible means of livelihood.

In 1836 she married Calvin Stowe, a professor in the seminary. They were far from wealthy, at times even poor, for Professor Stowe, rich in Greek and Latin and Hebrew and Arabic, was rich in nothing else. Though she had a household of little children, and often a few boarders, Harriet continued writing from time to time. Her first check was used to buy a feather bed. When a new mattress or carpet was needed, or the year's accounts wouldn't balance, she would send off a story, literally to keep the pot boiling.

Outwardly their life in Ohio was orderly and quiet, but every month occurred something stirring, even spectacular. There were fierce debates on the slavery question among the seminary students. Doctor Bailey, a Cincinnati editor who started a discussion of the subject in his paper, twice had his presses broken and thrown into the river. Mrs. Stowe's brother went about his news-paper work armed. Houses of colored people were burned and attacked; the shop of an aboli-tionist was riddled; free negroes were kidnapped. The Beecher family slept with weapons at hand, ready to defend the seminary. Many slaves es-caping from Kentucky sought refuge in the town, where the Underground Railroad helped them to reach Canada and safety.

It was impossible to live in Cincinnati and not be personally affected. Servants were hard to secure, especially for a household with slender means, though colored maids were available. The Stowes had a young negress from Kentucky who had been brought to Cincinnati by her mistress and left there. When a man came across the river hunting for her, meaning to take her back to slavery again, Mr. Stowe and Henry Ward Beecher drove the poor girl at night, in a severe storm, twelve miles into the country, where they left her with a friend until search for her was given over.

Colored boys and girls came to the classes Mrs. Stowe had for her own children. One little fellow was claimed by his former master, arrested and put up at auction. The distracted mother begged and pleaded for help. Harriet Beecher Stowe went out and raised the money to buy the child and give him back to his mother.

Pathetic incidents such as these were continually coming to the attention of the professor's family. In Cincinnati this New England woman had a real acquaintance with negroes, and was quick to note their peculiar characteristics. Unconsciously she was absorbing and assimilating pictures of slavery which later served a great purpose.

"What is there here to satisfy one whose mind is awakened on the subject?" she asked. "No one can have it brought before him without an irrepressible desire to do something, but what is there to be done?"

To find this something-to-do gradually became one of her chief thoughts, even though her domestic cares were almost overwhelming and her health suffered from the strain. The resources of the family did not increase. One year she was ill six months out of the twelve, yet she put up the stiffest kind of fight against the most disheartening odds. Whenever the household was in a comparative calm she would seize her pen and write some story or sketch. A delicate, highly, strung, little woman, with seven children on her hands, she wrote in the tumult of the living-room, with babies tumbling about her, with tables being set and cleared away, with children being washed and dressed, and everything imaginable in a household going on.

Doctor Stowe received a call to Bowdoin College, in Brunswick, Maine. Perhaps the family was glad to leave the excited atmosphere of Cincinnati where feeling on the slavery question was so inflamed, and live once more in the calm of New England. Yet for Mrs. Stowe it was not to remain for long a calm background.

On the journey north she stopped in Boston at the home of her brother Edward. The fugitive slave bill was being debated in Congress just at this time and everywhere the hearts of thinking men were stirred. Her visit came at the height of the fierce and fiery discussion of the proposed law which not only gave southern owners the right to pursue their slaves into free states, but forced the North to assist in the business. Her brother had received and forwarded fugitives many a time. She heard heartrending accounts of slaves recaptured and dragged back in irons, of children torn from their mothers and sold south —this breaking up of families offended her most of all.

Soon after the Stowes were settled in their Maine home a letter came from her sister-in-law in Boston.

"Hattie, if I could use a pen as you can, I would write something to make this whole nation feel what an accursed thing slavery is."

Reading this letter aloud to the family, when she came to that sentence Harriet Beecher Stowe rose, crushed the paper in her hand, and with a look on her face that her children never forgot, she exclaimed, "I will write something—if I live, I will!"

She was forty years old, in delicate health, overladen with responsibilities; a devoted mother, with small children, one still a baby; with untrained servants requiring supervision; with her pupils to be taught daily; and boarders to eke out the limited salary—her hands were full to overflowing. It seemed unlikely that she would ever do anything but this ceaseless labor. But her heart burned within her for those in bondage. The law passed and the fugitives were hunted out and sent back into servitude and death. The people of the North looked on indifferently. Could she, a woman with no reputation, waken them by anything she might write?

While at a communion service in the little church at Brunswick, like a vision the death of Uncle Tom on Legree's plantation came before her. Scarcely able to control her sobbing, she hurried home, locked herself in her room, and wrote it out, exactly as it stands now, in a white heat of passionate enthusiasm. She read it to her two little boys, ten and twelve years old. Through his sobs one of them said, "Oh, mamma, slavery is the most cursed thing in the world!"

Then she wrote the opening chapters and offered the manuscript to Doctor Bailey who had moved his paper from Cincinnati to Washington. He accepted it and arranged that it should be printed in weekly instalments—a dangerous method unless the story is completed before publication begins. With only fragments of her time to write, she sent off the necessary chapters each week, composed sometimes in pain and weariness, under almost insurmountable difficulties, seldom revised, sometimes not even punctuated. But the story was to her so much more intense a reality than any other earthly thing that the required pages never failed.

The subject possessed her. Her whole being was saturated with her theme. Her hot indignation was welling up, her deep pity was a part of her inmost soul. Day and night it was there in her mind, waiting to be written, needing but a few hours to bring it into sentences and paragraphs. She had been a guest at the Shelby plantation soon after her arrival in Cincinnati. Now, nearly twenty years later, she described the details of that visit with minutest fidelity—the humble cot of the negro, the planter's mansion, the funny pranks and songs of the slaves. Eliza's escape was suggested by the story of one of her own servants. Uncle Tom's simple honor and loyalty were characteristics impressed on her by the hus-

band of a former slave woman for whom she
wrote letters, a man who remained in bondage
rather than break his promise to his master and
so win his freedom. Topsy was a child in Mrs.
Stowe's mission Sunday-school class, who only
grinned in bewilderment when asked, "Have you
ever heard anything about God?" When the
teacher asked again, "Do you know who made
you?" the answer was, "Nobody as I knows on,"
the eyes twinkling as she added, "I 'spect I
growed." And Legree's plantation was pictured
to her in a letter from her brother Charles, who
went on a business trip up the Red River to an
estate where the slaves were treated with a brutal-
ity almost indescribable. Her own experiences
thus gave the personal touch that fires knowledge
into passion.

"My heart was bursting with the anguish excited by the cruelty and injustice our nation was
showing to the slave, and praying God to let me
do a little, and to cause my cry for them to be
heard. Weeping many a time as I thought of the
slave mothers whose babes were torn from them,
I put my lifeblood, my prayers, my tears, into

the book," was her own graphic description of its making.

The story was not so much composed by her as imposed upon her. Scenes and conversations and incidents rushed on her with a vividness and importunity admitting of no denial. She had no choice in the matter, the book insisted on getting itself into shape and could not be withstood.

Years afterward an old sea captain asked to shake hands with the author of *Uncle Tom's Cabin*.

"I did not write it," said the white-haired lady gently.

"You didn't?" he ejaculated in great surprise. "Why, who did, then?"

"God wrote it," she replied simply, "I merely did His dictation."

"Amen," said the captain reverently, and walked thoughtfully away.

The serial ran in the *New Era* from June of 1851 to the following April. When it was nearing completion a firm in Boston offered to print it in book form, but feared failure if it was much longer.

"I can not stop," was her answer, "until it is done."

Henry Ward Beecher told his sister his plans to work against slavery in Plymouth church.

"I too have begun to do something," was her reply; "I have begun a story trying to set forth the sufferings and wrongs of the slaves."

"That's right, Hattie. Finish it and I'll scatter it thick as the leaves of Vallombrosa."

But there was small need for his endorsement. It was soon published as a book. Would anybody read it, she asked herself doubtfully; the subject was so unpopular. She would help it make its way, if possible, and sent a copy to Queen Victoria, knowing how deeply she was interested in the abolition of slavery. Then this busy woman waited in the quiet Maine home to see what the world would say.

The first day three thousand copies were sold, ten thousand in ten days, over three hundred thousand the first year. The magazine had paid her three hundred dollars for the manuscript; the check for her first month's royalty was ten thousand dollars, when Professor Stowe had hoped the proceeds would buy her a new silk dress. There were translations into twenty different languages, forty editions in England, while the publishers lost count of the number in America. How restful for the tired overworked woman to have more than enough for her daily needs, to be free from the anxieties of poverty!

"Having been poor all my life," she said, "and expecting to be poor for the rest of it, the idea of making money by a book which I wrote just because I couldn't help it, never occurred to me."

Written with a purpose, a great underlying principle, *Uncle Tom's Cabin* is distinctly the work of a woman's heart, not of her head. And this explains the book's merits as well as its literary defects.

"But if critics find unskilful treatment," wrote George Sand, "look well at them and see if their eyes are dry when they are reading this or that chapter. The life and death of a little child and of a negro slave—that is the whole book. The affection that unites them is the only love story."

Yet this book met with a success that reads like a fairy tale. It was dramatized immediately, six London theaters playing it at the same time.

Learned reviews printed long notices of it, leading writers in America and England added their critical appreciation. Even those rating it low as a work of art called it a true picture of slavery. The common people accepted it eagerly, making it the most widely read book of modern times. It was one of the greatest triumphs in literary history, to say nothing of the higher moral triumph.

Its effect on the public was electric. The air, already charged with feeling, was ready to become impassioned. After its reading the Missouri Compromise was felt to be monstrous and impossible, enforcing the fugitive slave law absolutely out of the question. Throughout the North the book was received with acclamations. All classes, rich and poor, young and old, religious and irreligious, read it. No one who began it could remain unchanged. Echoes of sympathy came to the author from all parts of the land; the indignation, pity and distress which had long weighed on her soul seemed to pass from her to the readers of the book.

Some of the slaveholders Mrs. Stowe pictured as amiable, generous, just, with beautiful traits of character. She admitted fully their temptations, their perplexities, their difficulties. She thought the abolitionists would say, "Too mild altogether!" But the entire South rose against the book, in a hurricane of denial and abuse. The daily papers featured column after column of minute criticism which seemed to leave the book in tatters —its facts were false, its art contemptible, its moral tone slanderous and anti-Christian. Thousands of angry and abusive letters poured in on the author.

"*Uncle Tom's Cabin* met with such a universal praising," she said to one of her brothers, "that I began to think, 'Woe unto you when all men speak well of you!' But I have been relieved of my fears on that score. If there is any blessing in all manner of evil said falsely against one, I am likely to have it."

In the North a large element condemned the book no less severely—those who thought slavery just, who feared civil strife, who opposed abolition. But it was encouraging at least in this respect: The subject of slavery was now fairly up for inquiry before the public mind. The systematic efforts which had been made for years to prevent its being discussed were proving ineffectual. And on the whole the North accepted the story as a fair indictment of the national sin and as a sermon to them on their part in it.

For the moral sense of the people was awakened. The men who had viewed the subject with indifference became haters of the system. The sleepy church which had lagged behind in the rear of progress was stirred as if by a blast from the last trumpet. Politicians in Congress trembled, statesmen scented danger near. The unpopular reformers who had taken their lives in their hands, found their ranks reinforced by sturdy enthusiastic recruits. The story told the same appalling facts they had been stating in their meetings and printing in their papers, but the people would neither listen nor read. But Uncle Tom spoke with authority, and not as the scribes.

The marvel of its time, the wonder of succeeding generations of readers, this book was the beginning of the end of slavery. No other individual contributed so much to its downfall—Whittier's fiery lyrics, Sumner's speeches, Phillips' eloquence,

the sermons of Parker and the Beechers, all fell
short of the accomplishment of Harriet Beecher
Stowe. She now found herself the most famous
woman in the world. When she went to
Washington, after the Civil War had begun,
Abraham Lincoln on being introduced to her
asked, "What! are you the little woman that
caused this great war?" and then took her off to a
deep window-seat for an hour's talk.

Invited to England, Mrs. Stowe found her
journey there almost a royal progress. People
stood at their doors to see her pass by. Children
ran ahead of the carriage and offered her flowers.
"That's her," cried out the newsboys on the street,
"d'ye see the courls?" A national penny offering,
coming from all classes of society, was turned into
a thousand golden sovereigns and presented to
her, to be used for the cause of the slave. There
were many addresses and public meetings and
demonstrations of sympathy, and from the people
a perfect ovation. The great of the court, of
literary England, anti-slavery leaders, united to
pay her homage.

One of her gifts she brought back to America,

in order to complete its record. The Duchess
of Sutherland gave her a gold bracelet in the form
of a slave's shackles, inscribed "We trust it is a
memorial of a chain that is soon to be broken."
Its links bore the dates for the abolition of the
slave trade and of slavery itself in England and
her possessions. Later Mrs. Stowe had other
links marked for the ending of slavery in the Dis-
trict of Columbia, the Emancipation Proclamation,
and the constitutional amendment abolishing slavery in this country—changes due largely to her
work, two of these events coming within a decade
after *Uncle Tom's Cabin* was published.

After her return to America, Mrs. Stowe kept
on writing—sketches of her experiences abroad,
essays and stories of New England life, and a second slavery novel called *Dred,* which the critics
announced a greater book than *Uncle Tom's
Cabin,* but its popular success was less.

Her whole soul was bound up in the affairs
of the nation as the crisis of 1861 drew nearer.
She dreaded war, yet believed that it was the
red-hot iron that must burn away the nation's
disease.

"It was God's will," she said, "that this land, north as well as south, should deeply and terribly suffer for the sin of consenting to and encouraging the great oppressions of the south; that the ill-gotten wealth which had arisen from striking hands with oppression and robbery should be paid back in the taxes of war; that the blood of the poor slave, that had cried so many years from the ground in vain, should be answered by the blood of the sons from the best hearthstones through all the free states; that the slave mothers whose tears nobody regarded should have with them a great company of weepers, north and south, Rachels weeping for their children and refusing to be comforted; that the free states who refused to listen when they were told of lingering starvation, cold, privation, and barbarous cruelty as perpetrated on the slave, should have lingering starvation, cold, hunger, and cruelty doing its work among their own sons, at the hands of these slave masters with whose sins our nation had connived."

Her own son was among the first to enlist when Lincoln called for volunteers. "Would you have men say that Harriet Beecher Stowe's son is a coward?" he replied to a question about his going. And she received him back from Gettysburg with a wound in his head from which he never recovered.

From morning till night, all the days of the week, throughout the war Mrs. Stowe worked steadily. Years before she had written an appeal to the women of America, setting forth the injustice and misery of slavery, begging them to work together to have the system abolished. And when a strong party arose in England favoring the South, she wrote another appeal to her sisters there, which helped to crystallize public sentiment in favor of abolition and the North, to stop the English talk of recognizing the independence of the confederacy and of mediation. Its effect on the press and on Parliament was at once evident, and all over the kingdom resolutions were passed for the Union.

During the trying days of reconstruction she worked to secure full rights for the freedmen. Living in Florida for the winters, and in Connecticut in the summers, both north and south she helped to educate the negroes whom she had helped to free.

She still wrote well for many years, though she never achieved another exceptional success. Thirty books in all she published, some of them admirable, and then claimed a release from active service, saying she had written all her thoughts. But had Uncle Tom been her only hero, still would she live in the history of our country as foremost in the movement against slavery.

CHAPTER XII

JULIA WARD was born in New York City, and lived most of her life there and in Boston. Her father was a wealthy banker, with a fine sense of American noblesse oblige. Her mother, a woman of scholarly tastes, died when Julia was only five.

Mr. Ward gave his children every possible advantage—lessons in French and Italian and music, as well as the best English education; and the three daughters had as good a training as the three sons. Julia was an unusual child with a wonderful memory, and learned very quickly. She wrote poems, solemn poems, when a very little girl. At nine she listened at school to recitations in Italian and handed the amazed instructor a composition in that language asking to be allowed to join the class—and this request was granted, though the other pupils were twice her age.

Life was a serious thing to this child who was brought up very strictly, with duty and dignity constantly impressed upon her. She heard frequently stories of her ancestors—colonial governors, Revolutionary officers, Nathaniel Greene, and Marion, the "swamp fox of Carolina,"—the long line passed before the grave little girl, terrible as an army with banners; but always with the trumpet call of inspiration in the thought that they belonged to her.

When she was sixteen her brother returned from several years of study in Germany, and a new world was opened to her—German philosophy and poetry, and simultaneously New York society; for at once he made the Ward home one of the social centers of the city. Julia became the reigning favorite and won everybody by her beauty and charm, her tact and ready wit and good humor. She continued her studies regularly, translating German and French and Italian poems, reading philosophy and writing verses.

Visiting in Boston, she made the acquaintance of the literary group there—Longfellow, Emerson, Whittier and Holmes. Charles Sumner was her brother's intimate friend, and one day when he and Longfellow were calling on Miss Ward they suggested driving over to the Perkins Institute for the Blind.

They had frequently talked to her of its founder, Doctor Samuel Gridley Howe, the truest hero that America and their century had produced, and withal the best of comrades. The Cheval r, they named him, a Bayard without fear and withu reproach. She knew something of the six years he had spent in Greece, fighting during the war for independence and serving as surgeon-in-chief. She knew of his pioneer work for educating the blind, and of his marvelous achievement in teaching Laura Bridgeman—the little blind and deaf and dumb girl, the statue which he had brought to life.

When the three friends arrived Doctor Howe was absent, but before they had finished their tour of the building Sumner spied him from the window and called out, "There he is now, on his black horse." The young lady saw him, "a noble rider on a noble steed," and into her life he rode that day, like a medieval chevalier, in spite of the fact that he was forty and she only twenty-four, in spite of the fact that she had lived a gay social life and he was a serious reformer and philanthropist who believed that with the world so full of needy people no one had a right to luxury.

Life with a reformer husband was not always the care-free thing Julia Ward had known, but she had shipped as mate for the voyage, she once said with a merry laugh, and added, "I can not imagine a more useful motto for married life." She realized always that the deepest and most steadfast part of herself she owed to Doctor Howe. "But for the Chevalier, I should have been merely a woman of the world and a literary dabbler."

With all the cares and joys of a rich home life with her six children, she found time for study and writing. She published two volumes of verse, the first anonymously, but the secret could not be kept, for people declared that no one but Julia Ward Howe could be its author.

In addition to his work for the blind, Doctor Howe edited an anti-slavery paper called the

Boston Commonwealth, and his wife helped him with that task. Garrison, Sumner, Phillips, Higginson and Theodore Parker became their friends and co-workers. To balance the reformers, Edwin Booth, Holmes, Longfellow and Emerson were frequent guests, drawn by the magnet of Mrs. Howe's personality.

The slavery question became more and more acute, and soon the country was plunged into civil war. Every earnest woman longed to be of some immediate service to the nation and to humanity. Mrs. Howe was fired with the desire to help. Her husband was beyond the age for military duty, her oldest son was a lad, the youngest child two years old. She could not leave home as a nurse. She lacked the practical deftness to prepare lint and hospital stores. She seemed to have nothing to give, there was nothing for her to do.

If only her gift for verses were not so slight! If she could but voice the spirit of the hour!

During the autumn of 1861 Julia Ward Howe visited Washington. With friends she went to watch a review of the northern troops, at some distance from the city. While the maneuvers were going on, a sudden movement of the Confederates brought the pageant to a close. Detachments of soldiers galloped to the assistance of a small body of men in danger of being surrounded and cut off from retreat; while the troops remaining were ordered back to camp.

The carriage with the Boston visitors returned very slowly to Washington, for soldiers filled the roads. There were tedious waits while the marching regiments passed them. To beguile the time and to relieve the tense situation, they sang snatches of popular army songs, and one of these was *John Brown's Body*.

"Good for you!" called out the passing boys in blue, and joined in the chorus with a will, "His soul goes marching on."

"Mrs. Howe," asked James Freeman Clarke, who was in the carriage with her, "why don't you write some really worthy words for that stirring tune?"

"I have often wished to do it," she replied.

And that night her wish was fulfilled. Very early, in the gray of the morning twilight, she awoke and as she waited for the dawn the poem came to her, line by line, till the first stanza was finished. Phrase by phrase, and another stanza! The words came sweeping over her with the rhythm of marching feet. Resistlessly the long lines swung into place before her eyes. "Let us die to make men free, while God is marching on," and the *Battle Hymn of the Republic* was achieved.

"I must get up and write it down, lest I fall asleep again and forget it," she said to herself. In the half light she groped for pen and paper and scrawled the lines down, almost without look-ing—a thing she had often done before, when verses came to her in the night. With the words put down in black and white, safe from oblivion, she went to sleep again, saying drowsily to her-self, "I like this better than most things I have written."

The poem was published soon after in the *Atlantic Monthly,* but aroused little comment. The war, with alternate victory and defeat, en-grossed public attention. Small heed could be paid to a few lines in a magazine.

But an army chaplain in Ohio read it, liked it, and memorized it before putting down the *Atlantic*. Captured at Winchester, where he had delayed to help the doctors with the wounded, this chaplain was sent to Libby Prison, in Richmond. One large, comfortless room the Union men had, with the floor for a bed. The Confederate officer in charge told them one night that the South had just had a great victory; and while they sat there in sorrow old Ben, a negro who sold them papers, whispered to one prisoner that this news was false, that Gettysburg had been a great defeat for the South.

The word passed like a flame. Men leaped to their feet, and broke into rejoicings. They shouted and embraced one another in a frenzy of joy and triumph. And the fighting Chaplain McCabe, standing in the middle of that great room, lifted up his fine baritone voice and sang, "Mine eyes have seen the glory of the coming of the Lord." Every voice took up the chorus and "Glory, glory hallelujah, our God is marching on," rang through Libby Prison. You can imagine the effect of the tremendous uplift of the lines.

Released, the fighting chaplain began work for the Christian Commission and gave a lecture in the hall of representatives in Washington. As part of his recent experiences he told this incident of their celebration of the battle of Gettysburg, and ended by singing Mrs. Howe's poem, as only the man who had lived it could sing it. The great audience was electrified. Men and women sprang to their feet and wept and shouted. Above the wild applause they heard the voice of Abraham Lincoln calling, while the tears rolled down his cheeks, "Sing it again!"

McCabe sang it and the nation took up the chorus. The story of this lecture made the hymn popular everywhere. It was sung in all the homes of the North, at recruiting meetings and rallies. The troops sang it in bivouac at night, and on the march. The Union army seized on it as its battle cry and sang it as they went into action.

This song, which wrote itself in a wonderful moment of inspiration, embodied the very soul of the Union cause. Yet throughout its twenty lines there is no hint of sectional feeling. It was like an electric shock to the people of the

North, the call of a silver trumpet, the flash of a lifted sword. It inspired them with hope and courage, giving a new faith in the justice of God. The strength it brought to millions of men and women can·never be measured.

And in the world war of the twentieth century, somewhere in France, it was sung over and over. Phrase by phrase, the words fitting new conditions, as they fitted those of the sixties—the lightning of His terrible sword, the fiery gospel written in burnished rows of steel, the trumpet that shall never call retreat, sifting out men's hearts before His judgment seat, let us die to make men free—these apply in any warfare or crusade where men are fighting not for self, but for ideals.

After the war was ended Mrs. Howe continued to study, to write essays and poems, to give lectures, to serve in many great causes. But she is best remembered for the message which seemed to come to America, through her loving and so: · rowing heart, from God himself, in the *Battle Hymn of the Republic.*

CHAPTER XIII

MARY A. LIVERMORE

1821-1905

MARY ASHTON RICE was a little Boston girl, brought up very strictly. She was a restless active child, quick to learn at school, always enthusiastic over her tasks. A great favorite and a leader, she took the part of any unfortunate child in school; a cripple, a shabbily dressed youngster, one who was ridiculed because of her scanty luncheon, found friend and defender in Mary.

There were few playthings for the Rice children and Mary invented a wonderful game called "playing church." In the old woodshed they arranged logs for the pews and sticks of wood eked out the audience of children. Mary always conducted the services, praying and preaching with the greatest seriousness, while the others listened. And her father would say, "I wish you'd been a boy, child, we'd have trained you for the ministry." None of them ever dreamed that she would become a great public speaker and would often give addresses in churches.

Graduating from school at fourteen, she went to the Charlestown Female Seminary, and before the term closed was asked to take a position made vacant by the death of one of the teachers. Reciting and studying out of hours, she managed to complete the four-year course in two years and at the same time earned the money for this education.

Then she went as governess in the family of a Virginia planter. She had heard Lucretia Mott and Whittier lecture, and determined to find out for herself whether the facts of slavery were as black as they were painted. She came back from her two years in Virginia, a stanch abolitionist.

She served as principal in a Massachusetts high school for the next three years, and resigned to marry Doctor Livermore, a young minister whose church was near the school. She assisted in his parish work; she started benevolent and literary and temperance societies among the church-members; and she helped her husband edit a religious paper, after they moved to Chicago. She frequently wrote stories and sketches for eastern magazines, and she sat at the press table in the "Wigwam" when Lincoln was nominated for the presidency in 1860. With her writing, her three children, and a quiet, happy home life, doing the common duties of every day, it seemed impossible that Mary Livermore would ever be helping to make American history.

But Lincoln was elected, Sumter was fired on, the nation plunged into civil war, the president called for volunteers.

Summoned to Boston by her father's illness, Mrs. Livermore was in the station when the Massachusetts troops started south. The streets were crowded, the bells rang, the bands played. Women smiled and said good-by when their hearts were breaking. After the train had pulled out several women fainted and Mrs. Livermore stayed to help them.

"He has only gone for three months, you know," she said to one little mother.

"If my country needs him for three months or three years, I'm not the woman to hinder him," was the brave reply. "When he told me at noon to-day he'd enlisted I gave him my blessing and told him to go, for if we lose our country, what is there to live for?"

Seeing such partings Mary Livermore could not rest. She had no sons to send. What could women do to help?

"Nothing," was the answer from Washington when they offered their services; "there is no place for women at the front, no need for them in the hospitals."

The outbreak of the war found the North wholly unprepared. Hospitals were few and poorly equipped, nurses scarce and not well trained; there were no diet kitchens, no organized ways to supply medicines to the sick, to care for the wounded. Taxed to the utmost in every direction, the government could not meet all the urgent demands for hospital supplies. Relief societies sprang up everywhere, working individually, sending boxes to the troops from their special localities.

But what a waste in that haphazard method! Perishable freight accumulated till it was a serious problem. Baggage cars were flooded with fermenting sweetmeats and broken jars of jelly. Decaying fruit and demoralized cakes were found packed in with clothing and blankets. The soldiers were constantly moving about and many packages failed of delivery. The lavish outpouring of the generous people of the North meant for a time a lavish waste. If the men's answer to Lincoln's call was unparalleled, no less remarkable was the response of the women; but it needed to be systematized and organized like a great business. That was Mary A. Livermore's contribution to saving the Union.

To supplement the work of the federal government the Sanitary Commission was established. Mrs. Livermore was president of an aid society in Chicago which was one of the first to merge with the Commission. And from then till peace came she gave her time, her energy, her heart and mind and soul to the work of relief. She had enlisted not for three months, but for the duration of the war. With Mrs. Jane Hoge she served as organizer and executive not only for all the activities of Chicago and Illinois, but for the entire Northwest. Faithfully she worked to provide for

Mary A. Livermore had enlisted not for three months, but for
the duration of the war.

the sick and wounded soldiers abundantly, persistently, methodically.

What full and varied days she had for those
four years—opening a great sewing-room in Chicago where hospital garments were made by the
wives of soldiers, writing hundreds of letters with
news of missing men, establishing a system of relief for their families and for refugees, giving in-
structions and arranging transportation for
groups of nurses starting to the front, planning
ways and means to raise money and supplies, writing for her husband's journal and for other pub-
lications sketches of her "Sanitary" experiences,
supervising the four thousand aid societies under
the Chicago office, constantly visiting groups of
ladies to help them start the work, sending out
monthly bulletins to keep in close touch with these
branches, appointing inspectors to report on the
quality of food and water, and the sanitary arrangements in camps and hospitals, printing and
distributing to the army pamphlets on preserving
health in camp and emergency treatment, initiat-
ing and overseeing forty soldiers' lodgings—free
hotels for men passing back and forth separated

from their regiments—helping with a pension agency, a back-pay agency, a directory of more than two hundred hospitals, sending to the battle-fields surgeons and instruments, ambulances, anesthetics, and frequently going herself to see that the things reached the men and were efficiently distributed.

The work of the women of the Northwest she consecrated and organized, making them half-soldiers while she kept the soldiers half-civilian by bridging over the chasm between military and home life. She planned wisely, largely. She worked exactly, persistently. In a few months army surgeons were enthusiastic in their praise of the Sanitary Commission, where at first the whole scheme was regarded as quixotic, described as the fifth wheel of a coach, and reluctantly agreed to only because its plans could do no harm. And the people of the North accepted their larger methods and gave supplies to any hospital and any men needing them. The Commission became the great channel through which the bounty of the nation flowed to the army.

Every hour saw boxes arriving at the crowded

rooms of the Chicago branch, where the total force of workers was four. Supplies were unpacked, assorted, repacked, one kind in a box, and sent to Washington or Louisville, the gates to the South. A high standard Mrs. Livermore set for her aid societies—one box of hospital supplies every month, and this standard she upheld throughout the war. Such a rigid system was insisted on, in receiving and distributing their stores, that a very insignificant fraction was lost, the vouchers taken at every stage making it possible to trace them back to the original contributors.

Her first actual war experience was after the victory at Donelson. There was a cold rain during the first day's fighting which changed to sleet and snow with a bleak wind. There were no tents. The men bivouacked in the snow. Hundreds of them who fell were frozen to the ground and had to be dug out. The hospitals were not ready for such a stream of patients. There were few ambulances. In their bloody frozen uniforms wounded men were jolted over the hilly roads in springless carts, to be sent to St. Louis.

Mrs. Livermore spent three weeks in the different hospitals there and in Cairo, visiting every ward, reporting careless arrangements, happy to see great improvements on her second visit. Always the men greeted her gladly, stretching out their hands to touch hers, talking freely of home and friends.

A year later she was sent down the Mississippi with shipments of sanitary stores, to inspect every hospital from Cairo to Young's Point, opposite Vicksburg. Mud and water she found everywhere, swamp fever and malaria and scurvy. One group of hopelessly sick men she offered to take north with her, and Grant made this possible by cutting the red tape of the military régime.

The demand for hospital supplies increased steadily, as the army increased in numbers and in the scope of its operations. The Sanitary Commission expended fifty million dollars during the war, each battle costing about seventy-five thousand, and Gettysburg half a million. And in raising this vast sum Mrs. Livermore was one of the most efficient workers.

She planned a great Sanitary Fair in Chicago,

to raise twenty-five thousand dollars. The men laughed at such an impossibility. But the women went ahead. They hired fourteen of the largest halls in the city, and went into debt ten thousand dollars. They must have gone crazy, said the business men, and sent a committee to advise that the fair be given up, and adding that when they thought the money was needed they would contribute the twenty-five thousand. But the ladies thanked them courteously and continued with their plans.

Such a fair as it was, opening with a great parade, "the potato procession," the papers had called it, making sport of the scheme. The school children were given a holiday. Banks and stores were closed. Railroads ran excursions, bells rang, guns were fired, the whole city gathered to see the parade—children carrying flags, convalescent soldiers in carriages, captured standards of the Confederate armies, and farmers' wagons with mottoes such as "Our father lies at Stone River" and "We buried a son at Donelson." The flags on the horses' heads were edged with black. The women who rode beside son or husband were dressed in black. And when the parade stopped in front of Mrs. Livermore's house, the crowd was in tears.

The farmers gave great wagon loads of potatoes and cabbages and onions, for shipment to the soldiers. Live stock was sold at auction just outside the main hall. In manufacturers' annex were plows and reapers and stoves and trunks and washing machines, all for sale. There was a curiosity shop, an art gallery whose treasures were loaned for the fair, one hall for entertainments every evening—concerts, tableaux, lectures by Anna Dickinson, the girl orator. Dinner was served each day. When it was all over the women had cleared a hundred thousand dollars.

But the fair did far more than raise this large sum of money. It was a splendid demonstration of loyalty to the Union. It encouraged the soldiers. It kindled an electric generosity and a contagious patriotism, infusing into widely scattered groups of workers an impetus that lasted through the war. It captured the attention of the entire loyal North for weeks. Its success led to Sanitary Fairs in Cleveland, Boston, Pittsburgh, St. Louis, New York and Philadelphia.

Soon after the Chicago fair was over, Mrs. Livermore was asked to speak to an aid society in Dubuque, Iowa. She left on the night train, reaching the Mississippi River at a point where there was no bridge and travelers must cross by ferry. But the ice in the river had stopped the boats. She waited nearly all day. Could she keep her engagement? At last she saw two men starting out in a small rowboat, but they refused to take her.

"You'll be drowned," they said.

"I can't see that I shall drown any more than you!" was her reply, and finally they rowed her across. Her determination to accomplish whatever she undertook was one reason for her success.

She had expected to talk informally to a small group of women. To her dismay she found that great preparations had been made. The largest church in Dubuque was filled with an eager crowd, the governor and many noted men being present, and every county in Iowa represented. And her lecture was announced, "A Voice from the Front."

"I can't do it," she said. "I'm not a public speaker. What I had to say to a few ladies is not worthy to be called a lecture to this great audience. I can't do it!"

So it was arranged that Colonel Stone, with whose regiment she had spent some time near the line of battle, should take down brief notes of the talk she would have given to the aid society, and tell the story to the people. They had started into the church to carry out this plan when he said to her, "I've seen you at the front, I watched your work in the hospital, and I believe you're in earnest. I've heard you say you'd give anything for the soldiers. Now is the time for you to give your voice. Shall this opportunity be lost—or shall Iowa be enlisted for the work of the Sanitary Commission?"

"I will try," said Mary A. Livermore.

The sea of faces blurred before her. She seemed to be talking into blank darkness. She could not hear her own voice. But suddenly the needs of the soldiers crowded upon her mind, the destitution, sickness, suffering she had seen at the front,—and the people of Iowa must be roused to do their share. She thought she had spoken half an hour, it was nearly two hours. The audience listened spellbound, men and women weeping, every heart filled with a new patriotism.

"Now," said the governor when she closed, "Mrs. Livermore has told us of the soldiers' needs. It is our turn to speak, and we must speak in money and gifts."

Eight thousand dollars were pledged, five hundred barrels of potatoes, bushels of onions and anti-scorbutics of which the army was greatly in need. People stayed till eleven o'clock, and the leaders till one, planning for an Iowa fair which later cleared sixty thousand dollars.

That was the first public speech of the little Mary Rice who had preached to sticks of wood. But it was not the last. In hundreds of towns she spoke, raising thousands of dollars for hospital work and soldiers' homes, helping organize aid societies and fairs.

And after the war, from Atlantic to Pacific, in churches and colleges, in city and country, she lectured to crowded houses, talking on her war experiences in the "Sanitary," on temperance and woman's suffrage. A most popular speaker she was, achieving much for the various causes with which she was connected. But most of all she is remembered for the wonders accomplished in the many-sided work of the Sanitary Commission, whose efficient service helped to win the war.

CHAPTER XIV

BARBARA FRITCHIE

1766-1862

IN DECEMBER, 1766, a daughter was born in the house of a German immigrant, Nicolaus Hauer, in Lancaster, Pennsylvania, and she was named Barbara. She had four sisters and brothers. Their early years were spent in Pennsylvania and then the family moved to Frederick, Maryland.

Barbara went to school for a while in Baltimore. Her education was the best that could be obtained at that day, for she was "thoroughly well-read and could write." When she was ninety-two years old she scorned making her mark on business papers and proudly signed her name.

Barbara remembered the discussions that went on, when she was a very little girl, about the Boston tea party and the English taxes. She was nearly ten years old when the Declaration of Independence was signed. All her life long she talked with great pride of the success of the colonists. She remembered many scenes of the Revolution. Step by step she watched Washington's career and shared in the popular rejoicing when peace was announced. In 1791 Washington was entertained in Frederick and Barbara begged that her china be used in pouring the tea at the ball. And when Washington died and a memorial funeral was held in the town, she was chosen as one of the pall-bearers.

Frederick was a lovely little gem, set in a circle of historic hills, like Nazareth—an old town with narrow streets and lanes, and houses with queer roofs where the shingles had a double lap that made them look like old Dutch tiles. There was a market square in the center of the town, and on the outskirts the stone barracks built during the reign of Queen Anne, where Braddock met Washington and Franklin in council, and where prisoners were kept during the Revolution.

Here lived Barbara Fritchie, an active capable woman, known for her sturdy good sense, her incessant industry and her intense loyalty to her country. Literally she grew with its growth, watching its progress through the War of 1812, the admission of new .states, westward and ever westward expanding, till gold was discovered in California; and always the slavery question sinister and threatening in the background.

When Barbara was nearly forty she married John Caspar Fritchie, a glove maker. They lived in a little high-gabled story-and-a-half house on West Patrick Street, built of red brick penciled in white, with white shutters and two dormer windows in the long sloping roof. They owned two slaves, Nellie and Harry, who were so kindly treated that when freed they returned often, as children seek the home of their parents.

Her husband died in 1849 and Dame Fritchie, who never had any children, lived alone in the little house, busy with her many nieces and nephews, her knitting and her garden; a slight figure, under medium height, with small penetrating eyes, usually dressed in black alpaca or satin, with a starched muslin kerchief crossed on her breast, and a close white cap. She was always firm and decisive, and had indeed the reputation of a sharp tongue.

Then began the Civil War and Barbara, ninety-four years old, was noted for her fearless behavior and her intense outspoken loyalty, when loyalty was not the easiest matter in that border state. For Frederick had much to endure that winter. Soldiers of both armies were constantly in the way, skirmishes and duels were frequent in the narrow streets.

The flag was always flying from the Fritchie window and Dame Barbara kept busy, helping sick soldiers and cheering the despairing Unionists. "Never mind," she would say when news of reverses came, "we must conquer sometime." For stimulated by the glorious memory of what she had lived through, she had a supreme faith that the Union must survive. "It will never happen that one short life like mine shall see the beginning and the end of a nation like this." She would ask the shopkeeper, "How do matters look now?" If the reports were cheering her joy was evident; if sad, she would say, "Do not be cast down. We have seen darker times. Stand firm, it will all come right, I know it will. The Union must be preserved."

BARBARA FRITCHIE

Often the southern troops marched through Frederick, tired out, and stopped to rest on the porches of private houses. Once they halted in front of Barbara Fritchie's home, sat on her steps, and went to the spring near by for water. To all this she made no objection, but when they began to talk in a derogatory way of her beloved country, she was at the door in a moment and bade them move on, laying about her with her cane in the most vigorous manner, crying, "Off, off, you Rebels!" and clearing the porch in a few moments.

With victory alternating between North and South, matters dragged on until September of 1862, when Lee's advance troops under Stonewall Jackson spent a week in Frederick, to encourage recruiting for the Confederate army. Every Union flag was ordered hauled down, and according to one version of the story Barbara Fritchie, with the other loyalists, took down her flag and hid it in the Bible, saying that no Rebel would think of looking for it there.

Another story tells how on the morning of the sixth Dame Barbara's niece went to see her and

told her of a rumor that the soldiers would pass
through the town that day. Presently the child
ran in and called out in great excitement, "Aunt
Fritchie, the troops are coming!"

To the loyal old lady troops meant only one
army. She heard the sound of marching feet.
Picking up a silk flag she stepped out on the porch
and waved it at the men passing. Instantly a
murmur arose. A captain, riding up to the porch,
said kindly, "Granny, you had better take your
flag in the house."

"I won't do it, I won't," was her reply, as she
saw for the first time that the passing soldiers
were dressed in gray. Defiantly she shook the
flag. The excitement in the ranks increased.
Threatening murmurs arose. Another officer left
the line and said, "Old woman, put that flag away,
or you may get in trouble."

"I won't," she responded and waved it again.

Angry shouts came from the men. A third officer approaching warned her:

"If you don't stop that, you'll have that flag shot
out of your hand."

The captain, who was still standing near, turned

to him and said angrily, "If you harm a hair of
her head, I'll shoot you like a dog! March on,"
he commanded sternly, for some of the soldiers
had lifted their guns.

On the twelfth of September the southerners
left Frederick and the Union forces marched in,
to leave the following day for South Mountain
and Antietam. It was common talk among the
northern soldiers that some old lady had kept a
Union flag flying from her window during the
Rebels' possession of the town, and that it had
been fired on.

As the Federal troops were leaving the city
General Reno noticed a crowd of people in front
of Barbara Fritchie's home, reined in his horse
and heard the story. On being told that she was
more than ninety years old, he exclaimed, "The
spirit of 1776!" and his men gave a mighty shout
that echoed along the street. Some of the boys in
blue ran to the window and grasped her hand,
saying, "God bless you, old lady!" and "May you
live long, you dear old soul!"

The general dismounted to shake hands with
the aged heroine, who gave him some home-made

currant wine, served in the blue delft from which Washington had drunk. He asked if she would sell him the flag. This she refused to do, but gave him a bunting flag.

"Frank," he said to his brother as they rode away, "whom does she remind you of?"

"Mother."

The general nodded his head. The next day Reno fell at South Mountain, mortally wounded, and Barbara's flag was placed on his casket when it was sent north to his Massachusetts home.

Three months later Dame Fritchie died, at fourscore and sixteen, and was buried in the little graveyard of the Reformed Church in Frederick.

Her story was published in the newspapers and gained credence in Maryland and in Washington. It was accepted as a fitting symbol of a real and great emotion of the people. Mrs. Southworth, the novelist, hearing it from friends and from a neighbor who was a connection of the Fritchie family, sent it to Whittier, adding, "This story of a woman's heroism seemed as much to belong to you as a book picked up with your autograph on the fly-leaf."

BARBARA FRITCHIE

Within a fortnight after its receipt the Quaker poet, in his most heroic mood, wrote his Barbara Fritchie ballad, remarkable for its lofty patriotism. Though he had no military training his lines are full of the spirit of army life, the tread of marching soldiers, the orders short and sharp, a stirring setting for the courageous act of an old lady of ninety-six.

"It ought to have fallen into better hands," Whittier wrote to Mrs. Southworth. "If it is good for anything thee deserves the credit of it."

The poem was sent to the *Atlantic Monthly,* whose editor replied, "Enclosed is a check for fifty dollars, but Barbara's weight should be in gold!"

The ballad was, and is, most popular through the North, for it belongs in the class which the world will never willingly let die. But it aroused great enmity in the South where people bitterly resented the statement that a favorite general had ordered his men to fire on an old lady. There were many denials of all the details of the story, some from members of the Fritchie family—that Jackson did not pass the Fritchie house, proved by statements from his staff; that Barbara had waved her flag only to welcome the Union army, and the incident had been blended with the story of Mrs. Quantrell, a loyal school-teacher who did wave the flag in sight of the Confederates; that no such person as Barbara Fritchie had ever lived in Frederick!

Said Whittier years later, "There has been a good deal of dispute about my little poem. That there was a Dame Fritchie in Frederick who loved the old flag is not disputed by any one. If I made any mistake in the details there was none in my estimate of her noble character and her loyalty and patriotism. If there was no such occurrence, so much the worse for Frederick City."

Across the town from the little churchyard where John and Barbara Fritchie lie buried is the monument marking the grave of the author of *The Star-Spangled Banner*. And in both cemeteries the flag floats out, signaling the one to the other, fulfilling the lines of the Quaker poet:

"Over Barbara Fritchie's grave
Flag of freedom and union, wave!
And ever the stars above look down
On thy stars below in Frederick town."

CHAPTER XV.

CLARA BARTON

1821-1912

CLARISSA HARLOWE BARTON was born on December twenty-fifth, in an old farmhouse in Worcester County, Massachusetts. Her grandfather had fought through the Revolution, her father in Mad Anthony Wayne's campaigns against the Indians. Clara listened to many a stirring story of the dangers they had met. As they fought their battles over again, she learned her country's history and loved it passionately.

The older Barton children were her teachers and very rapidly indeed she learned. For she went to school at three, able to spell words of three syllables, but so shy she could not answer questions. Her athletic brother David, whom she admired greatly, taught her to ride.

"Learning to ride is just learning a horse," said he.

"How can I learn a horse?" asked the little sister.

"Just feel the horse a part of yourself, the big half for the time being. Here, hold fast by the mane," and David lifted her up to a colt's back, sprang on another himself and away they galloped down the pasture—a mad ride which they repeated often, till she learned to stick on. In after years when she rode strange horses in a trooper's saddle, for all-night gallops to safety, she was grateful to David for those wild rides among the colts.

Strong in body, alert in mind, Clara Barton grew up, never free from shyness unless she was busily at work. "The only real fun is doing things," she would say. She helped milk and churn, she learned to drive a nail straight, to deal with a situation efficiently, with quick decision.

When she was eleven David was seriously in jured by a fall from the roof of a new barn, and was for two years an invalid. At once Clara took charge, her love and sympathy expressed in untiring service. In a moment she was changed from a lively child, fond of outdoor sports, to a nurse

calm and cheerful, full of resources, no matter
how exacting the doctors' orders were, no matter
how much David was suffering. The sickroom
was tidy and quiet. Clara was clear-headed, equal
to every emergency, always at her post, nothing
too hard for her to do well and promptly, if it
would make her brother more comfortable. For
those two years she had not even one half-holiday,
so her apprenticeship was thoroughly served.

"That child's a born nurse," the neighbors
would say. And the doctors, agreeing, praised her
tenderness and patience. Years later thousands
of men echoed David's words when he spoke of
her loving care.

But these two years made her more sensitive
and self-conscious. Her shyness and unhappi-
ness made her a real problem to her mother.

"Give her some responsibility," advised a wise
family friend, "give her a school to teach. For
others she will be fearless."

Far ahead of girls of her age in her studies, at
fifteen Clara Barton put up her hair and length-
ened her skirts and went to face her forty pupils.
"It was one of the most awful moments of my

life," she described it long afterward. "I could not find my voice, my hand trembled so I was afraid to turn the page. But the end of that first day proved I could do it."

Her pluck and strength won the respect of the big rough boys, who tried her out on the playground and found she was as sturdy as they. That school was a great success, and for sixteen years she taught, winter and summer.

In Bordentown, New Jersey, no school was possible, she heard, because of the lawless children who ran wild on the streets. The town officials were convinced it was hopeless, no use to make the experiment. Here was something to be done, it challenged her!

"Give me three months, and I'll teach for nothing," she proposed, her eyes flashing with determination.

In a tumbledown old building she began with six gamins, each of whom at the end of the day became an enthusiastic advertisement for the new teacher. At the close of the school year she had an assistant, six hundred children on the roll, and a fine new building was erected, the first public school in the state. For Clara Barton had a gift for teaching, plus a pioneer zeal.

When her voice gave out she went to Washington for a rest and secured a position in the patent office. So she was at the capital when the conflict long threatening between North and South developed into civil war. Sumter was fired on. The time for sacrifice had come.

In response to Lincoln's call for volunteers Massachusetts sent men immediately, and on the historic nineteenth of April one regiment was attacked in the streets of Baltimore by a furious mob. With a good many wounded their train finally reached Washington and was met by a number of sympathetic women, Clara Barton among them. In the group of injured soldiers she recognized some of her old pupils and friends. At the infirmary she helped dress their wounds. Nothing was ready for such an emergency. Handkerchiefs gave out. Women rushed to their homes and tore up sheets for bandages. This was Clara Barton's first experience in caring for wounded soldiers.

She wanted them to have the necessities, and all

the comforts possible. So she put an advertisement in a Worcester paper, asking for supplies and money for the wounded men of the sixth regiment, and stating that she would receive and give out whatever was sent. Overwhelming was the response of Massachusetts. The food and clothing filled her apartment to overflowing and she had to rent space in a warehouse.

This work made a new person of the shy Clara Barton who had been a bundle of fears. This was no time to be self-conscious. Here was a great need, and she knew that she had the ability to meet it.

South of Washington battles were going on. Transports left each day with provisions for the army of the Potomac, returning with a load of wounded soldiers. Clara Barton went to the docks to meet them. She moved about, bandaging here, giving medicine there, feeding those weak from the long fighting and lack of nourishment, writing letters home, sick at heart when she saw men who had lain on the damp ground for hours, whose fever had set in, for whom her restoratives and dressings and tender care were too late.

If only wounds could be attended to as soon as the soldiers fell in battle, she knew that hundreds of deaths could be prevented. She must go to the front, to the very firing line, though it was against all tradition, against all army regulations, against public sentiment. For many weeks she met only rebuffs and refusals, always the same reply: "No, the battle-field is no place for a woman. It is full of danger!"

True—but how great was the need of the men at the front, how great the need of each soldier's life for the nation! Help must be brought to them when they fell. She laid her plan before her father who said, "If you believe that it is your duty, you must go to the front. You need not fear harm. Every true soldier will respect and bless you."

Without a doubt then she determined to persist until she received permission. At last she was able to put her request to Assistant-Quartermaster General Rucker and asked him for a pass to the battle front.

"I have the stores, give me a way to reach the men."

"But you must think of the dangers this work will bring you. At any time you may be under the fire of the enemy's guns."

"But," was her answer, "I am the daughter of a soldier, I am not afraid of the battle-field." She described to him the condition of many of the men when they reached Washington and added earnestly, "I must go to the front, to care for them quickly."

The passport was given her and through the weary years of the war she stayed at her post—giving medicine to the sick, stimulants to the wounded and dying, nourishing food to men faint from loss of blood. Working under no society or leader she was free to come and go. On sixteen battle-fields, during the hot, muggy summer days of the long siege of Charleston, all through the Wilderness campaign, in the Richmond hospitals, there was no limit to her service. And from her first day on the firing line she had the confidence of the officers and their help and encouragement. Wherever there were wounded soldiers who had been under her care, Clara Barton's name was spoken with affection and with tears.

Through the weary years of the war Clara Barton stayed
at her post.

CLARA BARTON

In as far as was possible, word of coming engagements was sent her in advance, that she might be ready with her supplies. At Antietam while shot was whizzing thick around the group of workers, she ordered her wagons driven to an old farmhouse just back of the lines. Between the tall rows of corn, into the barnyard, the worst cases were carried. For lack of medical supplies the surgeons were using bandages of cornhusks.

Her supplies quickly unloaded, Clara Barton hurried out to revive the wounded, giving them bread soaked in wine. The store of bread ran out, she had left only three cases of wine. "Open them," she commanded, "give us that, and God help us all!" for faster and faster soldiers were coming in. She watched the men open the cases. What was that around the bottles? Cornmeal! She looked at it closely; yes, finely ground and sifted. It could not have been worth more if it had been gold dust. In the farmhouse they found kettles. She mixed the cornmeal with water and soon was making great quantities of gruel. All night long they carried this hot food up and down the rows of wounded soldiers.

On one of these trips, in the twilight, she met a surgeon tired and disheartened. He had only one short candle left, and if men's lives were to be saved, the doctors must work all night. "Heartless neglect and carelessness," he stormed. But Miss Barton had four boxes of candles in her stores, ready for just such an emergency.

Near that battle-field she remained until all her supplies were gone. "If we had had more wagons," she reported to General Rucker, "there would have been enough for all the cases at Antietam."

"You shall have enough the next time," he responded. And the government, recognizing the value of her service, gave her ten wagons and sixty mules and drivers.

Her work succeeded because she had initiative and practical judgment and rare executive ability and the power of managing men. When her drivers were rebellious and sulky, showing little respect for orders that put them under a woman, she controlled them just as she had the rough boys in her school. Once she prepared a hot dinner and asked them to share it. After she had cleared away the dishes and was sitting alone by the fire, awkward and self-conscious they came up to her.

"Come and get warm," she welcomed them.

"No'm, we didn't come for that," said the leader. "We come to tell you we're ashamed. Truth is, lady, we didn't want to come. We knew there was fightin' ahead, an' we ain't never seen a train with a woman in charge. Now we've been mean and contrary all day long, and here you've treated us like we was the general and his staff, and it's the best meal we've had in two years and we shan't trouble you again."

The next morning they brought her a steaming hot breakfast and for six months remained with her, through battles and camps and marches, through frost and snow and heat, a devoted corps of assistants, always ready for her orders. They helped her nurse the sick and dress the wounded and soothe the dying, and day by day they themselves grew gentler and kinder and more tender.

Once Clara Barton worked for five days and nights with three hours of sleep. Once she had a narrow escape from capture. Often in danger it seemed as though she had a special protection that she might save the lives of others. Stooping to give a wounded soldier a drink of water, a bullet whizzed between them, tearing a hole in her sleeve and ending the boy's life.

She gave her help to men who had fought on either side. They were suffering, they needed her, that was enough. No man is your enemy when he is wounded. She leaned over a dying officer in a hospital; a Confederate looked up into her kind face and whispered:

"You have been so very good to me. Do not cross the river, our men are leading you into an ambush. You must save yourself."

But his warning was unheeded when later that day the hero-surgeon who was opening an emergency dressing-station across the river, asked her help. She went over to Fredericksburg where every stone wall was a blazing line of battle. A regiment came marching down the street. She stepped aside. Thinking she must be a terrified southerner, left behind in their hurried flight, the general leaned from his saddle to ask:

"You're alone and in great danger, madam. Do you want protection?"

"Thank you, but I think"—Clara Barton looked up at the ranks of soldiers marching past— "I think, sir, I'm the best protected woman in the United States!"

"That's so, that's so," cried out the men and gave her a great cheer that was taken up by line after line till it sounded like the cheering after a victory.

"I believe you're right, madam," said the general, bowing low, and galloped away.

Over the battle-field a sharp wind was blowing. The suffering men lay shivering and half frozen in the bitter cold. Some were found famished under the snow. Clara Barton had all the wounded brought to one place and great fires built up. But that was not heat enough to warm them. What to do? She discovered an old chimney not far away. "Tear it down," she ordered, "heat the bricks and place them around the men." Soon she had kettles of coffee and gruel steaming over the fires, and many a life she saved at Fredericksburg.

As the war drew to an end President Lincoln received hundreds and hundreds of letters from anxious parents asking for news of their boys. The list of missing totaled sixty thousand. In despair the president sent for Miss Barton, thinking she had more information than any one else, and asked her to take up the task. A four years' task it proved to be. She copied infirmary and burial lists. She studied records of prisons and hospitals. At Andersonville she laid out the national cemetery and identified nearly thirteen thousand graves. She succeeded in tracing and sending definite word of thirty thousand men. From Maine to Virginia the soldiers knew her. Through the whole country her name became a household word.

Her strong will had held her body to its work during the long war and for this tracing service afterward. Then the doctors insisted she must rest and sent her to Switzerland for change of scene. After a month when she was beginning to feel some improvement, she had callers one day representing the International Red Cross Society.

"What is that?" asked Clara Barton.

And they explained—how a Swiss, visiting the

battle-field of Solferino and seeing thousands of
French and Austrians wounded, inadequately
cared for, had planned a society for the relief of
soldiers. Its badge, a red cross on a white
ground, would give its workers protection from
both armies, and they would help all persons
without regard to their race or religion or uni-
form—exactly the principle on which she had been
working, and to-day the very heart of the Red
Cross plan. Already, they said, the society was
formed and twenty-two nations had joined it.
But the United States, though invited twice, had
done nothing. They asked her help.

Three days afterward the Franco-Prussian
War began and soon Clara Barton was again
at the front. With the German army she entered Strasburg after the siege. On every hand
were sick and wounded soldiers, women and children homeless and ragged and starving. Relief
work started, she went to Paris on the outbreak
of the revolution there. And this work made
her enthusiastic about the Red Cross. For at
once she felt the difference—she saw the new
society accomplish in four months, with system

and trained workers, what our country had failed to do in four years. What a contrast—supplies in plenty, wounds dressed at once, cleanliness, comfort, wherever the white flag with the red cross was flying, instead of mistakes, delays, needless suffering, lives sacrificed. She said to herself, "If I live to return to America, I will try to make them understand what the Red Cross and the Geneva Treaty mean."

She succeeded, though it was a task of years. She found officials indifferent, hard to convince, clinging to the tradition and prejudice that forbade any alliance with foreign countries, and saying, "Why make plans for another war? We'll never have it!"

But in March, 1882, the treaty was signed. Clara Barton became the first president of the American Red Cross Society, an office she held for twenty-two years. It was her suggestion that they be prepared to meet any emergency and give relief in time of peace as well as war. It was her influence that carried this American amendment in the International Red Cross Congress.

CLARA BARTON

Many have been the calamities where the Red Cross has given aid—two wars, floods in the Ohio and Mississippi Rivers, the Texas famine, the Charleston earthquake, the disaster at San Francisco, Florida's yellow fever, the Johnstown flood, forest fires—these are a few of the urgent calls in our own land; and abroad the sufferers in the Russian and Chinese famines, in Armenia and South Africa, bear witness to her care.

Eighty years old, she went herself to Galveston. At seventy-seven McKinley sent her to carry relief to the starving Cubans. And during the Spanish War she nursed American and Cuban and Spanish soldiers, once in a storm repeating her Antietam experience with hot gruel!

Vast sums of money, poured out by the generous American people, were placed at her disposal for relief to the suffering and destitute. A sufficient sum in ready cash she always kept on hand, in case a telegram came when the banks were closed; for there must be no delay in the Red Cross's starting on its mission of mercy.

The world over Clara Barton was known and loved and honored. The German emperor gave her the order of the iron cross, which at that time had been awarded only for heroism on the battle-field. Queen Victoria herself pinned an English decoration on her dress. The Duke of Baden, Serbia, the Prince of Jerusalem all gave her honors; and her home was decorated with the flags of all the nations.

Dying at ninety, Clara Barton, retiring and bashful, had given fifty years of service to suffering humanity, working always on the firing line. David's born nurse became head nurse to all the nation. The angel of the battle-field, as the soldiers loved to call her, became the country's angel of mercy.

And in the Red Cross Society, building perhaps better than she knew, Clara Barton gave the opportunity for every American citizen, man or woman or little child, to share in her work of love and mercy.

EPILOGUE

Thus ends the story of these women who helped to make the history of our country. It is a record of courage and of service, of splendid achievement. And these fifteen women by no means tell the whole story. The contribution of each could be duplicated, in less degree, many times. They are but typical of countless women who have been true American patriots.

The exploring and settling of our country lasted for three centuries, the building of the nation is not yet finished. There is work for the women of to-day, if they would be worthy inheritors of these fifteen, to shape the present true, for the generations to come after. Making history offers a wide range of service, for heroism wears many forms, as these brief stories show. But it is of the greatest importance to the nation that its ideals of heroism shall be high and true.

Every woman can be a soldier faithful, brave and loyal. We of to-day and of to-morrow must stand shoulder to shoulder with the inspired women of the past, to express the best in womanhood, to work for the highest ideals.

BIBLIOGRAPHY

BIBLIOGRAPHY

CHAPTER I

Eggleston—*A First Book in American History,* 23-41.

Holland—*Historic Girlhoods,* 92-106.

Jenks—*Captain John Smith.*

Seelye and Eggleston—*Pocahontas.*

Smith—*The Story of Pocahontas and Captain John Smith.*

Sweetser—*Ten American Girls from History,* 1-35.

CHAPTER II

Bouvé—*American Heroes and Heroines,* 13-31.

Brooks—*Dames and Daughters of Colonial Days,* 1-29.

Eggleston—*The Beginners of a Nation,* 326-341.

Foster, ed.—*Heroines of Modern Religion,* 1-22.

Hart—*American History Told by Contemporaries,* I, 382-387.

CHAPTER III

Harrison—*The Stars and Stripes,* 60-64.

Horner—*The American Flag.*

Schauffler—*Flag Day,* 50-58 and 61-66.

Tappan—*The Little Book of the Flag.*

BIBLIOGRAPHY

CHAPTER IV

Brooks—*Century Book of the American Revolution*, 87-89.
Hemstreet—*The Story of Manhattan*.
Ullmann—*Landmark History of New York*.
Wilson—*New York Old and New*.

CHAPTER V

Bouvé—*American Heroes and Heroines*, 120-128.
Brooks—*Century Book of the American Revolution*, 130-135.
Journal of American History, 5:84 (1911).
Stockton—*Stories of New Jersey*.
Sweetser—*Ten American Girls from History*, 71-85.

CHAPTER VI

Brooks—*Dames and Daughters of Colonial Days*, 133-167.
Herbert—*The First American—His Homes and His Households*.
Lossing—*Mary and Martha Washington*.
Wharton—*Martha Washington*.

CHAPTER VII

Brady—*Border Fights and Fighters*, 151-163.
Purcell—*Stories of Old Kentucky*.

BIBLIOGRAPHY

CHAPTER VIIi

Brooks—*First across the Continent.*
Dye—*The Conquest.*
Holland—*Historic Adventures,* 21-58.
Journal of American History, I:468 (1907).
Laut—*Pathfinders of the West.*
Lewis and Clark—*Journals.*
Schultz—*Bird Woman* (written by a man adopted
    by the Blackfeet Indians, from accounts given
    him by friends of Sacajawea).

CHAPTER IX

Bolton—*Famous Leaders among Women,* 123-158.
Bouvé—*American Heroes and Heroines,* 171-180.
Brooks—*Dames and Daughters of the Young Re-
    public,* 1-42.
Holland—*Historic Girlhoods,* 203-216.
Madison—*Memoirs and Letters.*
Tappan—*American Hero Stories,* 224-230.
Todd—*The Story of Washington.*

CHAPTER X

Bolton—*Girls Who Became Famous,* 33-49.
Foster, ed.—*Heroines of Modern Religion,* 88-114.
Hallowell—*James and Lucretia Mott—Life and
    Letters.*
Morris—*Heroes of Progress in America,* 219-225.

BIBLIOGRAPHY

CHAPTER XI

Adams and Foster—*Heroines of Modern Progress,* 89-119.

Bolton—*Girls Who Became Famous,* 1-17.

Crowe—*Harriet Beecher Stowe: Biography for Girls.*

Fields—*Life and Letters of Harriet Beecher Stowe.*

Stowe—*Life of Harriet Beecher Stowe* (by her son).

Wright—*Children's Stories in American Literature,* 188-202.

CHAPTER XII

Adams and Foster—*Heroines of Modern Progress,* 178-214.

Bolton—*Famous Leaders among Women,* 272-303.

Bristol—*Life of Chaplain McCabe,* 192-203.

Howe—*Reminiscences.*

Parkman—*Heroines of Service,* 117-147.

Richards and Elliott—*Julia Ward Howe* (by her daughters).

Wade—*The Light Bringers,* 142-171.

Wright—*Children's Stories in American Literature,* book 2, 212-221.

CHAPTER XIII

Bolton—*Girls Who Became Famous,* 50-67.

Livermore—*My Story of the War.*

BIBLIOGRAPHY

Livermore—*The Story of My Life*, chapter 28.
Our Famous Women, 386-414.
Whiting—*Women Who Have Ennobled Life*, 53-85.

CHAPTER XIV

Bookman, 13:418 (1901).
Pennsylvania German, 1906.
Southern Historical Society Papers, vol. 27.

CHAPTER XV

Adams and Foster—*Heroines of Modern Progress*, 149-177.
Barton—*The Red Cross in Peace and War*.
Bolton—*Successful Women*, 198-223.
Epler—*Life of Clara Barton*.
Parkman—*Heroines of Service*, 59-85.
Sweetser—*Ten American Girls from History*, 143-173.
Wade—*The Light Bringers*, 64-111.

INDEX

INDEX

Barton, Clara: nurse at eleven, 190-1; success as teacher, 191-3; cares for first wounded soldiers in Civil War, 193; distributes supplies, 194; receives permission to go to front, 195-6; war record, 196-201; appointed to search for missing, 201-2; serves under Red Cross in Franco-Prussian War, 203-4; starts Red Cross in America, 204; its president for twenty-two years, 204; service in disasters, 205; honors paid her, 205-6.

Battle Hymn of the Republic, 159-63.

Beecher, Henry Ward, 132, 136, 144.

Bishop (Washington's body-servant), 56-8, 67.

Burr, Aaron, 45, 104-5.

Chaboneau, Toussaint, 81-7, 91, 96-8.

Dale, Governor, 11, 12.

Declaration of Independence, 111, 120, 170.

Fritchie, Barbara: saw four wars, 179-82; marriage, 181; her loyalty and faith when Civil War broke out, 182; troops in Fredericksburg, 182-3; different versions of flag story, 183-5; Whittier's poem, 186-8.

Fugitive slave law, 128-9, 138-40, 146.

Garrison, William Lloyd, 118, 122, 125, 131.

Hamilton, Alexander, 45, 63.

Harlem, battle of, 45-6.

Howe, General, 41, 43-6.

INDEX

INDEX

INDEX

Powhatan, 2-6, 8-13.
Putnam, Israel, 41-6.

Red Cross, 202-6.
Rolfe, John, 11, 12, 15.
Ross, Betsy: apprenticed, 30; marriage, 30; reputation as needlewoman, 31, 33; widowed, 32; five-pointed star, 35; her flag adopted by Congress, 35-7.
Ross, Colonel George, 33.

Sacajawea (Bird-woman): taken prisoner, 80-1; marries Chaboneau, 81; meets Lewis and Clark, 81-2; engaged as interpreter, 82; birth of son, 82; heroine of expedition, 83-4; saves papers and instruments, 84-5; illness, 85-6; escape from cloudburst, 86-7; guides expedition, 88, 92-3; meets friend and brother, 89-90; persuades tribe to help white men, 90, 92; bargaining with Indians, 91; resourcefulness, 94; rapid return trip, 95-6; bids farewell to leaders, 96; later years and death on Indian reservation, 98-9; memorials, 99-100.
Sanitary Commission, 168-72.
Smith, John, 2-8, 14.
Stanton, Elizabeth Cady, 122.
Stars and Stripes, 34-7.
Stowe, Harriet Beecher: early interest in compositions, 133-4; moves to Cincinnati, 134; marries Professor Stowe, 135; discussions over slavery, 135-7; her own experiences with negroes, 136-7, 141-2; writing, 135, 138; excitement over fugitive slave bill, 138-9; how

INDEX

34947

DATE	
DEC 2 1 '73	
NOV 2 2 1978	
DEC 1 1 1978	
JY 14 '83	
GAYLORD	